Embroidery Illusions

Embroidery Illusions

Gary Clarke

SALLYMILNER
PUBLISHING

Dedication

I would like to dedicate this book to my parents. To my mother, who didn't teach me embroidery, but has given me a love of design and detail. Her passion for gardening has not rubbed off, but her fondness for floral design has. To my father, who died in the early weeks of starting this book, for giving me the freedom of reaching beyond that which is comfortable and expected.

As always, I give thanks to God for the inspiration that is so abundant all around us and the abilities that He has given.

First published in 2003 by
Sally Milner Publishing Pty Ltd
PO Box 2104
Bowral NSW 2576
AUSTRALIA

© Gary Clarke 2003

Design: Anna Warren, Warren Ventures Pty Ltd
Editing: Anne Savage
Photography: Tim Connolly

Printed in China

National Library of Australia Cataloguing-in-Publication data:

Clarke, Gary.
Embroidery illusions.

ISBN 1 86351 304 3.

1. Embroidery. 2. Embroidery - Design. 3. Embroidery - Patterns. I. Title.

746.44

10 9 8 7 6 5 4 3 2 1

Contents

Introduction

Embroidery worked on fine transparent organza, stretched over a frame, creates an illusion of stitching suspended in air — as if embroidered on glass.

This form of embroidery presents another illusion — it looks as though it is difficult, due to its fine appearance and the seemingly delicate nature of the materials used. Every illusion has its secrets, however. The first secret here lies in stretching the organza, which is surprisingly strong, and attaching it firmly to a frame before the embroidery begins. The shadow cast by the embroidery onto the background is the second secret that completes the illusion of floating threads.

Stitching techniques are surprisingly straightforward, being limited to simple stab stitches, as more complex stitches like bullions are difficult to execute on the tightened organza.

Disciplines similar to those of watercolour painting are used. Despite the overall effect of transparency, the work still needs to have a detailed focal point grounding it. The detail then fades away into abstract or transparency.

Stitchery can be used exclusively, but this kind of embroidery lends itself well to combination with other mediums, giving the work a new dimension. In several of the designs I have incorporated shadow backgrounds created by cardboard cutwork, in others a painted background; in three designs I have also incorporated found objects. Like all things in life there is a balance, and there may come a point where I suppose this kind of work can no longer be called embroidery — it's your choice how far you go.

The background, with the shadows created on it, is most important in this form of embroidery, and in its own way carries as much artistic weight as the stitchery itself.

This book is not simply a project book, although there are

twenty projects with detailed instructions. I hope that it will also be seen as a teaching book. Each project has some new aspect, some idea which you can go on to apply to other designs of your own. I have also supplied a number of unworked design ideas at the back of the book which I hope will stimulate and inspire you to venture out beyond what can be seen into what can be imagined.

I trust you will enjoy exploring the possibilities.

God bless, Gary.

Stitch Glossary

Blanket stitch

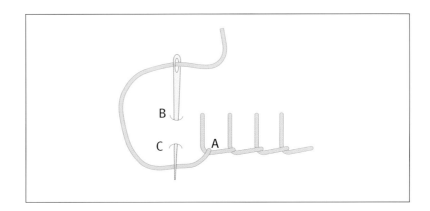

Bullion stitch

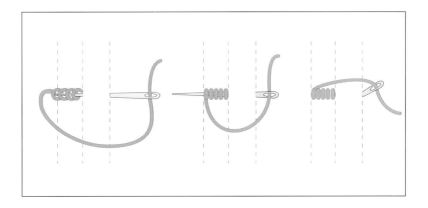

This stitch is difficult worked on tight organza. However, if worked with both hands using a table to support the work it will be easier.

Colonial pistil stitch

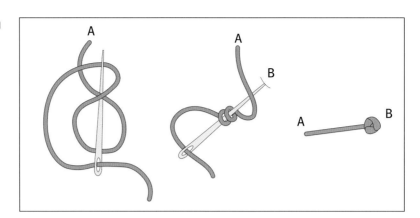

Couching

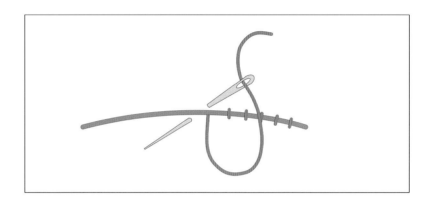

Detached
buttonhole

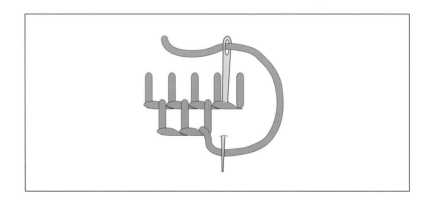

French knot

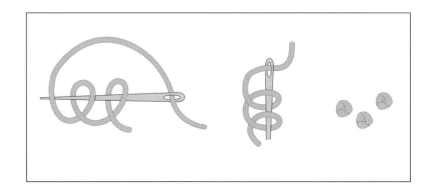

Half cross-stitch

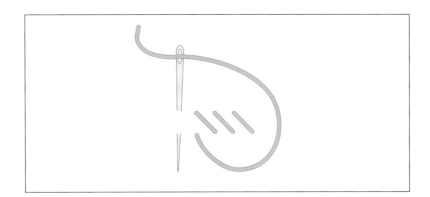

Long stitch

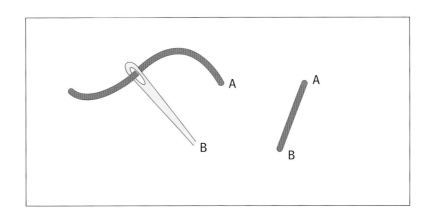

Pistil stitch

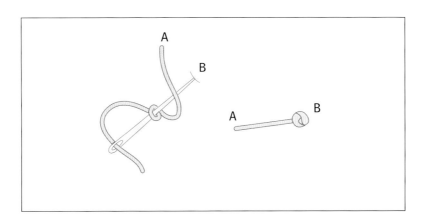

Running stitch

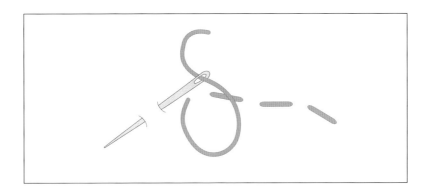

Satin stitch

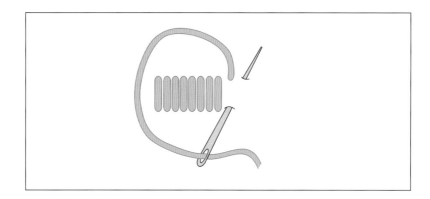

Split stitch

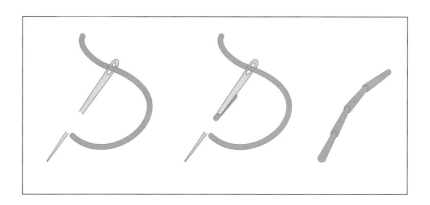

Straight stitch

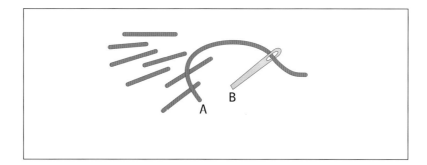

The knot

Because of the transparent nature of organza it is necessary to secure the thread as invisibly as possible. Fasten a conventional knot on the surface of the work away from current work. Come up through the fabric and take a small stitch. Stitch back into the stitch several times. When finished, cut away the waste knot. To finish off in the open, repeat the process.

Special effects from stitch variations

Many of the designs use slight variations on regular embroidery stitches which combine with the translucence of the stretched organza to provide special effects. You will find references to this section when the variations are called for in the designs.

Running stitch 50-50

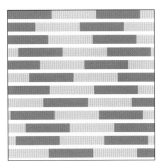

The aim with this stitch is to take advantage of the colour change that is created when the stitch is seen travelling underneath the organza. Keep the stitch on the surface a similar length to the one underneath.

Running bottom stitch

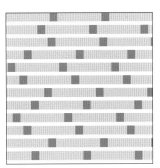

When the stitch travels under the organza it becomes lighter in colour. In this instance a light shaded look is created with the stitch predominantly underneath. The top stitch gives an added dimension of a little pin spot.

Running top stitch

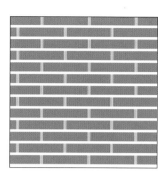

To create strong dense colour on top of the fabric, have the top stitch predominant with only a tiny stitch underneath. This will create a satin stitch style of stitch. This stitch has an advantage over satin stitch in that it can be manipulated to curves when needed.

Running damask stitch

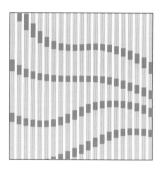

By varying the length of the top stitch to that of the one underneath, will create a different look. A damask look can be created by defining the design with the top stitch while the stitch underneath fills in. all these stitches make patterns inside patterns.

Running long and short stitch

Straight and tapering filling can be achieved by loosely filling a shape with long running stitches. Divide the space left with more long running stitch, keep doing this till the area is filled. This will give a long and short effect and a thread direction that will enhance the design.

Crossed
shadow stitch

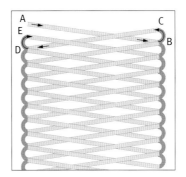

Shadow embroidery takes on a new dimension on organza. Fasten the thread underneath at A. take the thread along underneath to B. bring the thread to the surface at B and back down at C. take the thread along underneath to D. bring the thread to the surface at D and back down at E.

Flat satin stitch

This can look very much like satin stitch. The difference is that it lies flatter to the surface, with no sense of padding. This technique can be used with stitches close together or sparsely spaced.

Sculpturing
satin stitch

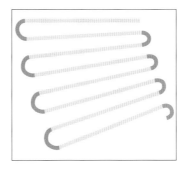

The flattened satin stitch can also be worked in reverse, having the main stitch underneath the fabric. With both variations, curving and shaping is achieved by decreasing and increasing the sides.

**Shadow
satin stitch**

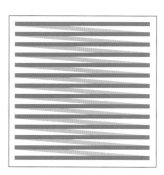

The traditional satin stitch with the thread travelling underneath the fabric. This stitch too can be opened up to reveal the diagonal stitch travelling underneath the fabric. Satin stitch is more padded than the flattened satin stitch and therefore also adds texture.

**Couching
variations**

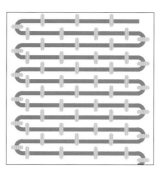

| hidden under | travelling alongside |
| the thread | the thread |

Couching usually uses two threads, one a cord that will not pass easily through the fabric, and a normal sewing thread. The two threads can be of similar colour or contrasting for effect. The sewing thread is crossed over the couching thread and taken diagonally underneath it, or over the couching thread and travelled alongside it.

Running
top stitch

As organza is so fine one is able to take very small stitches on the underside; when stitching a line in running stitch it appears to be continuous.

Special notes on
satin stitch

cotton

silk

rayon

All threads have different degrees of flexibility;
you can use this characteristic to your advantage.

If you have had problems with satin stitch in the past here are a few tips that you might find helpful.

The finer the fabric, the closer and more even is the stitch required (and organza is a very fine fabric).

Tension is very important. Keep in mind the word 'lay'—that is, lay the thread down, don't pull it.

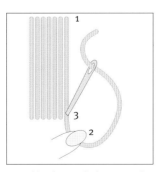

Positioning a stitch accurately
1 Find parallel line
2 Hold in place with finger
3 Pierce through the thread to secure

When it is essential to get the right angle, or for the stitches to be absolutely parallel, use the thread as a string line to determine the lay of the next stitch; when the positioning is right, hold it in place, then pierce the thread with the needle to ensure it does not move right or left.

It is often helpful to work an outline in a stitch like running stitch, split stitch or chain. Putting a foundation stitch down first helps in two ways: first, it helps sew the threads of the fabric together, making it more stable to work, and secondly, it gives a firm edge so that the edge of the satin stitch is also firm.

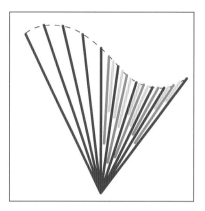

When filling in an area that tapers or has an irregular shape, tackle the situation similar to working long and short stitch. Start in the middle with a long stitch from top to bottom — this will establish a good pivot point for the threads to fan out from. From there, fan out stitches at double to triple spacing on either side of the first stitch. Next, divide each of the spaces left with another stitch (this will be a little shorter). Keep dividing the spaces until all the area is covered. This form of filling gives a guaranteed result with stitches that follow the flow of the design.

Materials and Techniques

Threads

Although most threads are suitable for this kind of work, the thicker silks such as Madeira and Au Ver à Soie are perfect. One strand of these threads is thicker than one strand of stranded cotton, providing the advantage of having a substantial thickness of thread while escaping the difficulties encountered in using multiple threads, such as tangling and twisting.

Silk threads

Silk is the best thread to use. It is strong and comes in many thicknesses and lustres.

Madeira silk

Medium lustre, 4 strands, and medium thickness (1 strand = 1 ½ strands of 6-strand cotton). Smooth to work with. Well packaged. Excellent for the main body of the work.

Au Ver à Soie Silk

Several different lustres. Several different thicknesses, from fine to a high-lustre baby cord. A comprehensive and beautiful colour range. Very smooth to work with.

Gumnut Silk

Dull to medium lustre. Variegated and excellent for colour grading. Colours are clear and natural. The thread is coarser than most silks, yet still soft, giving a nice texture. I suggest that the skein be unwound and then plaited so as to straighten the thread.

YLI Silk

Medium lustre, 6 strands. A fine thread used mainly for highlights.

Cotton threads

Cotton must be used in short lengths; around 10 in (25 cm). It is best used for small highlights and wears better if worked through areas of worked silk. Gary Clarke Candlewicking 2-ply Soft Cotton is used in some of the projects, stranded cottons in some others.

Metallic threads

Hand metallics

Hand metallics add opulence. They are great for both highlights and texture. Most, however, are only suitable for couching as they are too rough to pass through the organza.

Machine metallics

Machine metallics are better suited for stitching through the fabric as their surface has been made smooth for the sewing machine. They are ideal for couching down the thicker, rougher threads. Multiple strands can be used to add texture.

Golden Threads Cou

A metallic filament wrapped around a fibre core. Golden Threads have a full range of metallic threads.

Silk ribbon

Silk ribbon can be used to great effect, but remember, the longer the ribbon the more damage it will suffer. Use in short lengths.

Needles

I like to use a quilting needle for organza work wherever possible. Because it is fine it offers little resistance to the fabric. I particularly like the large-eye quilting needles by John James and Richard Hemming, available from most retailers.

Organza fabric

As there are many brands and blends of organza available, from a multitude of outlets, I won't specify any particular one, just outline the qualities to look for.

I prefer a Japanese synthetic organza which has a light sheeny lustre (not shiny). Although it is very fine, one can easily see the individual threads, and there is no dominant direction to the weave — that is, the warp and weft have equal weight. When stretched it has a cloudy transparency. Avoid the shiny types of organza that when stretched often form 'lines' due to a prominent direction in the weave — this will result in a wave effect surrounding the design that detracts from the embroidery. A good bridal supplier should have what you need.

Note It is important with organza, more than with any other fabric, that you work with the light behind you, in such a position that it falls directly on the front of the design. If the light is in front of you so that it shines through from the back of the work, the organza will appear transparent and be very hard to work on. A strong light directed to the front of the design at night will make working with organza very easy.

Frames

Start your project by making two lightweight frames from pine or similar wood. A good profile is ¼ in x 2 in (5 mm x 5 cm), a fairly standard pine measurement. Over one frame you stretch the organza; the second is for the background. Make sure the frames are well glued and V-stapled, as the stretched organza exerts considerable pressure. The intended embroidery area, plus an allowance for a mount, determines the size of the frames. The size required is specified for each design, the dimensions given being for the external measurements of the frame.

The second frame has a piece of ⅛ in (3 mm) white foam core fixed to it, of the same dimensions as the frame.

Stretching the organza

Fasten double-sided tape around the outer edge of one of the pair of frames. Lay the frame in the centre of a piece of organza approximately 2 in (5 cm) larger on all sides than the frame.

Fold one end of one edge onto the double-sided tape and staple. Stretch the organza along the length of the tape on that side and press it firmly to the tape, stapling as you go.

Repeat the procedure on the opposite side, this time also stretching the organza across the frame. There is no need to try aligning the weave of the fabric.

Repeat the procedure until all four sides are stuck and stapled. On completion the organza should be as tight as a drum skin. Cover the staples and raw organza edges with masking tape to prevent fraying and add strength to the stretching.

Transferring the design

Transferring the design is easy, as all that is needed is to place the framed organza over the design plan and trace around it with either a soft black lead pencil or a fine-tipped water-erasable pen.

Be aware that the pencil lead may make marks on light-coloured threads as you embroider. If you use a water-erasable pen, wait for it to dry before you start to work; because the 'ink' doesn't soak into the organza it tends to stay wet for some time.
A word of caution Water-erasable pens are not suitable for use in conjunction with the fusible webbing called for in some designs.

Heat-fusing

Some designs call for colour photocopying a section of the design and heat-fusing it to the stretched organza in the frame.

Having made a colour copy, fuse the printed side of the copy to the organza with Vliesofix fusible webbing. If the design has to be cut out, do so after the fusible webbing has been applied.

Using the paper backing from the fusible webbing as an ironing shield, iron the top of the organza. 'Fill' the frame with something solid—a book or a block of wood, perhaps, topped with an appliqué mat—to give support to the stretched organza and the iron. Use a heat setting sufficient to fuse the webbing without melting the organza.

Working side

Normally the embroidery is worked from the concave side of the framed organza. The depth of the frame gives the space required for the glass to clear the work when the external frame is added.

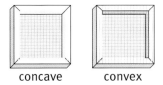

concave   convex

Designs incorporating fusible webbing (for example, Golden Magnolia on page 33) must be worked on the convex side of the framed organza.

Design notes

The designs in this book are simple, yet most will stand a little embellishment if you wish to make them more your own. Projects like the seahorse possibly have more embellishment than you might wish to include—in that case you might like to work it in a similar manner to the monkey.

Backgrounds

The background often carries a substantial responsibility in the effectiveness of the design. I use two different types.

The first type is very simple, using the background of the second frame as a surface onto which to project the shadow of the embroidery. In some cases the background may include a coloured wash or pattern, or a cut paper design. As a rule it is most effective to leave the background in light colours to emphasise the contrast of the shadow from the embroidery.

The second type of background, most often used in this book, is the stage. A standard stage is made of a square of ⅛ in (3 mm) white foam core the same size as the embroidered area, with a smaller piece beneath it to raise it a little. The stage may be left white or decorated. It can also be cut and shaped, as seen in a few designs.

The stage internally frames the work, similarly to the external mounts usually used. It also plays with the shadows; it casts a shadow itself and splits the shadow cast by the embroidery so that it is seen on two levels.

Putting the work together

When the embroidery is finished it is time to put together all the elements.

Make sure that all threads are secure and no loose ends are showing from the front.

Take the second frame, covered on one side with a piece of foam core.

Place the embroidery on top of the second frame. Look for the shadow cast by the embroidery, the definition of the embroidery against the background, and whether it is giving the effect you are looking for.

At this stage you may want to add a stage to bring the background closer to the embroidery. This will make the shadows stronger and the edge of the embroidery sharper.

This is when you add to the background, with papercuts and the like.

When all is glued together on the background, put the embroidery and background together. Tape them together so they become one unit (work frame). Use tape so that it can be removed should the background move or foreign objects become trapped between the background and the organza.

Take the work frame to a commercial framer for the external frame to be fitted. Double mounts and small beaded edges can look effective. Do not use non-reflective glass as this will soften the contrast of the shadow and take away from the lustre of the thread.

Hanging and lighting

Because the shadow is so important in this form of embroidery it is essential that the lighting is correct when the finished work is hung.

Hang the embroidery on a wall in such a position that the light falls on it at an angle; this will cast the better shadow.

If lighting artificially, have the light hit the embroidery at an angle also, to cast the best shadow.

Threads are identified by manufacturers' colour codes. The colour descriptions for threads are supplied by the author.

Grand Old Oak

The oak leaf and the acorn are both examples of God's love of embellishment, and found on the same tree. With the contrast between the dark knurled base and the shiny polished wood look of the nut, the acorn is a pleasure to the touch and to the sight. Just as the acorn, the leaf is far from plain as well, with an almost frilled appearance. The look is beautifully brought together with the delicate greens of lichen and bright green moss growing on the trunk of the oak. Worked in muted earthy tones, this design gives an opportunity to try several variations of the same stitch and demonstrates the subtleties that can be achieved with organza.

Requirements

2 frames 12 ½ in (32 cm) square
organza to cover one frame
⅛ in (3 mm) foam core for background and stage
brown corrugated cardboard to cover stage
Madeira Silk 018: Oak Green 1508, Polished Wood 2210, Bark 2113
Au Ver à Soie perlée: Lichen Green 718
Delica beads DBR 371
twig (found object)

Stitches

Satin stitch, running stitch, detached buttonhole

Transferring the design

Make two frames 12 ½ inches (32 cm) square. Stretch organza onto one frame as detailed on page 21.

Transfer the design onto the framed organza. Centre the frame, organza side down, onto the pattern and trace with a soft black lead pencil or water-erasable pen (see page 21).

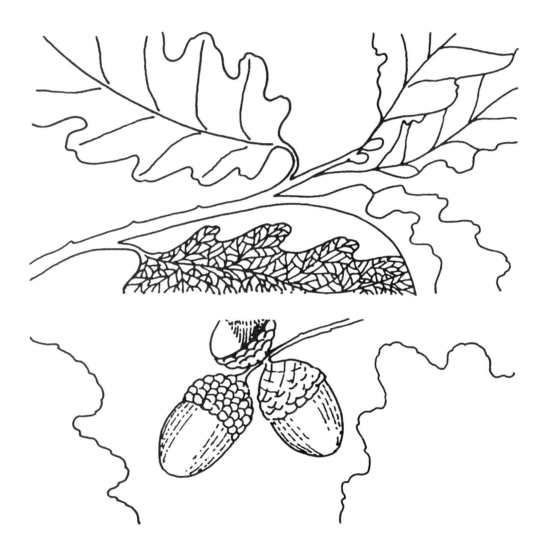

Tracing outline (same size)

Stems

Using one strand of Madeira Bark 2113, work the stems in running stitch.

More thread above the organza than below

Leaves 1, 2, 3, 4

Using one strand of Madeira Oak Green 1508, work leaves 1, 2, 3 and 4 in satin stitch, as indicated in the four stitch diagrams.

Leaf 1: The same amount of thread above as below the organza. Open up the stitch to double spacing.

Leaf 2: More thread above the organza than below. Open up the stitch to double spacing.

Leaf 3: The same amount of thread above as
below the organza.
Close up the stitching to form close satin stitch.

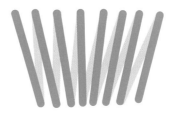

Leaf 4: The same amount of thread above as below
the organza. Open up and fan the stitch.

Using one strand of Au Ver à Soie perlée Lichen Green 718, work
a running stitch around the outside edge of leaf 4.

Leaf 4: The same amount of thread above as below the organza

Leaf 5

Work a running stitch around the outside edge of leaf 5 with one
strand of Au Ver à Soie perlée Lichen Green 718.

Leaf 5: More thread below the organza than above

To fill leaf 5, work a buttonhole stitch into the running stitch (not through the fabric). Work around the inside of the leaf. When back to the beginning, work into the previous buttonhole stitch. To finish off, lace both sides together with a buttonhole stitch.

Acorn nuts

Using one strand of Madeira Bark 2113, work a running stitch down each side of nut 1. Fill in the centre with running stitch reversed from the outside stitch.

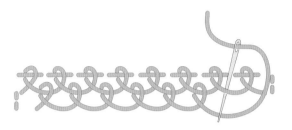

Outside of acorn: More thread above the organza than below

Filling: More thread below the organza than above

Using one strand of Madeira Polished Wood 2210, work nut 2 in the same manner.

Highlight and shade both acorns with surface stitching in Madeira Polished Wood 2210.

Acorn caps

Acorn cap: The same amount of thread above as below the organza

Using one strand of Madeira Oak Green 1508, work a small split stitch around the tops of the two nuts, then 2 rows of stitching around the edges of the three caps. Fill in the caps with a lattice effect created by a running stitch, as below.

Now, using one strand of Madeira Oak Green 1508, work a shadow satin stitch to fill in the empty cap, following the diagram.

Using Delica beads DBR 371, sew a bead into the gaps in the lattice in the cap of acorn 1.

Using one strand of Madeira Oak Green 1508, work a running stitch as above to create the lines of shading at the bottom right and left of the design.

Finish with one strand of Madeira Bark 2113, working small buds in padded satin stitch on the stem at the top right of the design.

Background

The background in this design is a simple stage covered with a piece of corrugated cardboard. Use a sharp craft knife and a metal rule to ensure the edges of the cardboard are cut cleanly. See Backgrounds, page 23.

Foreground

Carefully stitch a suitable twig, very light in weight, and preferably with a little lichen growing on it, over the gap in the embroidered design.

Golden Magnolia

Magnolias bear magnificent flowers, especially *Magnolia denudata*. A cold climate tree, it is quite rare, hard to propagate and expensive to buy. It is worth a little effort, however, for in full bloom it is truly inspiring to see. Even when not in flower its large leaves and substantial trunk put it in a class of its own. Although I have not used the flower's true cream colour in this embroidery, I have tried to keep its aristocratic character.

The colour in this design comes from appliquéd gold organza, the number of layers giving the varying depths of colour to the petals. The appliqué is edged in a simple split stitch of soft silk cord. The opulence of the silk and organza is enhanced by the amber coloured glass beads sewn into the lattice-stitch centre of the flower.

Requirements

2 frames 12 ½ in (32 cm) square
organza to cover one frame
gold organza 5 in (12 cm) deep across width of fabric, for petals, stage and tie
Vleisofix 5 in (12 cm) square
⅛ in (3 mm) white foam core for background and stage
Au Ver à Soie perlée: Settlers Green 658, Colonial Green 718
Delica beads DBR 604

Stitches

Split stitch, running stitch

**Transferring
the design**

Make frames and stretch organza onto one frame as detailed on page 21.

Transfer the design onto the framed organza. Centre the frame, organza side down, onto the pattern and trace with a soft black lead pencil (do not use a water-erasable pen for this design, as the marks would become permanent when the fusible webbing is ironed into place; see page 22). Note this design is worked convexly (see page 22).

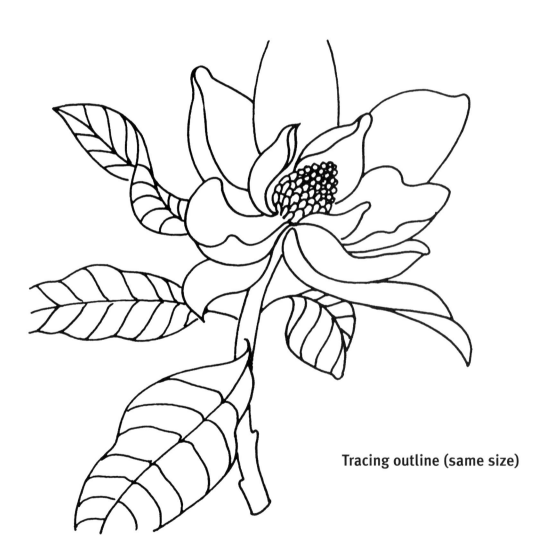

Tracing outline (same size)

Flower

Fuse one side of the gold organza with fusible webbing following the manufacturer's instructions. Place an appliqué mat under the organza to prevent it sticking to the ironing surface as it comes through the organza. Remove and retain the paper backing. The full flower is cut out of the 5 in (12 cm) fused square; there is enough left over to cut out the extra pieces to layer the darker petals.

Cut out the full flower and iron it onto the pencil outline on the framed organza, filling the frame to support the iron as described on page 36.

Cut out the shaded petals only from the remaining fused organza, following the diagram as a guide, and iron in place on the full flower.

Key:
green 718 ——
light green 658 —

Using Au Ver à Soie perlée Settlers Green 658, work a split stitch around the light petals as indicated.

Using Au Ver à Soie perlée Settlers Green 718, work a split stitch around the dark petals as indicated.

Leaves

Using Au Ver à Soie perlée Colonial Green 718, work a running stitch around the outside of the leaves.

More thread above the organza than below

Then define the veins in running stitch, using Au Ver à Soie perlée Colonial Green 718.

More thread below the organza than above

Centre of flower

Add single beads to the lower portion of the latticework in the centre of the flower

Stem

Using Au Ver à Soie perlée Colonial Green 718, lay long couched stitches close together (like satin stitch) to form the stem. Couch down with the same thread.

Again using Au Ver à Soie perlée Colonial Green 718, work 4 threads diagonally across the bottom of the stem in a zigzag, following the photo for guidance.

Background

In keeping with the opulent nature of this design, the stage is treated in a slightly more lavish manner than usual, as you can see from the photograph. The usual square of foam core is cut a little oversize, at 5 ¼ inches (13 cm) square, then a 5 ¼ x 1 ¼ inch (13 x 3 cm) strip is glued to the bottom front, and another of the same dimensions glued to the top underneath (as shown in the diagram).

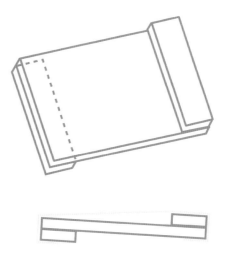

The stage is then covered tightly with some of the extra gold organza, and a twisted length is secured to the left-hand side. Finish by securing the stage to the background with craft glue.

Seahorse

The seahorse is a fascinating creature, so unlike other marine dwellers that it is in a class of its own. Seahorses are difficult to keep in captivity as their seawater needs to be kept very fresh. This particular species has an interesting shape but is very bland in colour, so to add interest I have used the colours of the sea to shape it.

This design is an example of adding found objects to embroidery. This has no rules, and how the design is treated will be determined largely by the found objects that are used. Why not begin collecting small things that can be added to embroidery? They look good in the embroidery plus look interesting as a collection in jars. Pebbles, cones, lichen, leaves and twigs all look great as features in embroidery. The seahorse design is made up of shells and couched cord. You will really enjoy the ease of couching and the freedom of adding found objects.

Couching is a very under-utilised stitch which can be used to great effect. One has several options when choosing the sewing thread—to complement or contrast, to be seen or not to be seen. In this case I chose Golden Threads Cou 371 Blue Opal for the couching thread and Madeira Mermaid Blue 1107 for the sewing thread. This gives little stitches of brighter blue mingled in among the predominantly green-blue of the opal thread.

Requirements

2 frames 12 ½ in (32 cm) square

organza to cover one frame

15 in (40 cm) blue organza for background

⅛ in (3 mm) white foam core for background and stage

Madeira silk 018: Mermaid Blue 1107, Seahorse Tan 2114

Au Ver à Soie perlée: Neptune Green 15

Golden Threads Cou 371: Blue Opal

Delica beads DBR 380
shells
craft glue
sheet of wavy corrugated cardboard

Stitches
Couching, running stitch

Transferring the design

Make 2 frames 12 ½ in (32 cm) square. Stretch organza onto one frame as detailed on page 21.

Transfer the line drawn design onto the framed organza. Centre the frame, organza side down, onto the pattern and trace with a soft black lead pencil or water erasable pen (see page 21).

Tracing outline

Shells

Lightly glue the shells to the design with craft glue, and allow the glue to dry completely before you begin the embroidery. If you don't, the glue will ruin your needle.

Note Test the glue on the organza before you start to make sure it does not dissolve the organza.

Seahorse

The next step was to work a running stitch around the outline of the seahorse, and the skeleton-like segments that define the body, using Au Ver à Soie perlée Neptune Green 15.

The seashells must be incorporated into the embroidery in such a way that they become one with it. To this end, couch over them to make it appear that it is the thread which holds them to the organza, using Au Ver à Soie perlée Neptune Green 15.

To begin, thread a darning needle with the couching thread, Golden Threads Cou 371 Blue Opal (just the tip of the thread in the needle). Take the needle through the fabric so that the tip of the thread is just seen on the back. Fasten the couching thread down with the sewing thread, Madeira Mermaid Blue 1107.

Couch along a similar path to the green silk running stitches. Use less of the couching thread than of the green silk, wherever possible laying it alongside the silk.

For the eye, lay the couching thread around it in a coil. When it is necessary to change direction and a sharp corner is needed, loop the thread into a right angle. The couching stitches will need to be closer together going around tight corners.

Embellish the embroidery with a few beads around the eye and scattered between the shells.

To create the mane, use Madeira Seahorse Tan 2114, working long loops through the organza.

Background

Make a standard foam core stage 5 ½ in (13 cm) square and glue a square of corrugated card the same size to the front. Mark, then cut a 4 ½ in (11.5 cm) square from the centre of the stage. Lay a piece of blue organza over the cut-out square. Reassemble the stage, turning the frame shape 90 degrees and fitting it around the organza-covered square, sandwiching the organza as if in an embroidery hoop. Trim the edges of the organza with pinking shears, about ⅜ inch (1 cm) out from the edge of the stage, and mount the stage as usual. Refer to the photograph for guidance.

You may wish to add strips of blue organza about 1 in (2.5 cm) wide running down the left side and across the bottom of the design.

Lily

Lilies are without doubt among the most majestic of plants. In all ways they are out to impress; their size, shape and colour are unmatched. The vibrant green stamens of the flowers, and the young foliage, enhance the pure colours of the petals. In this particular case the thread inspired the embroidery, the beautiful copper cord echoing the character of the lily. This design is predominantly couched, with a running stitch background in light copper mirroring the stitching in the petals.

Requirements

2 frames 12 ½ in (32 cm) square
organza to cover one frame
⅛ in (3 mm) white foam core for background and stage
Madeira 018: Red Lacquer 0402, Palace Brown 2113, ecru
Madeira 019: Dynasty Green 1540, Emperor's Lime 1580
Golden Threads Cou: Copper 371
Rajmahal Silk TMTA: Light Copper

Stitches

Couching, satin stitch, running stitch, detached blanket stitch

Transferring the design

Make two frames 12 ½ inches (32 cm) square. Stretch organza onto one frame as detailed on page 21.

Transfer the design onto the framed organza. Centre the frame, organza side down, onto the pattern and trace with a soft black lead pencil or water-erasable pen (see page 21).

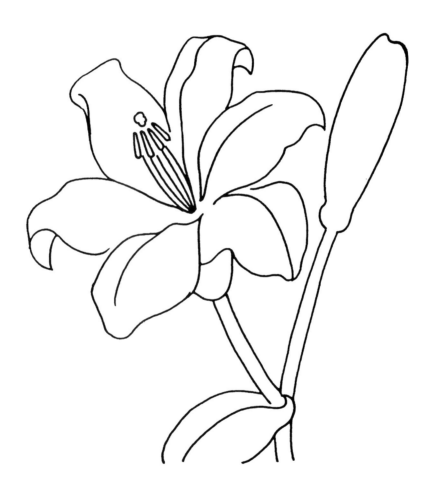

Tracing outline (same size)

Flower

Using one strand of Cou Copper 371 and one strand of Madeira Red Lacquer 0402, couch each of the petals.

Place the tip of the couching cord in a darning needle, draw approximately ¼ in (5 mm) of cord through the organza, and stitch fast the end to the organza. Make the stitches as small as possible, using Red Lacquer 0402 silk. At the completion of each petal, finish off the same way you started. Work from the outside of the petal to the middle.

To add body to the petals, work the sewing thread alongside the couching thread (refer to page 17).

Add shading to the petals with Madeira Palace Brown 2113 and Madeira ecru, placing a brown running stitch on the shadow side of the petal and an ecru stitch on the light side.

**Stamens
and pistil**

Using two strands of Madeira Emperor's Lime 1580, work four long straight stitches for the stamens. Bend the outside two slightly with a couching stitch.

In one strand of Madeira Palace Brown 2113, work a ¼ in (6 mm) bullion stitch at the top of each stamen.

Above the stamens, using one strand of Madeira Emperor's Lime 1580, work three small vertical straight stitches and cross them with three horizontal straight stitches. This is the padding for the pistil.

Work satin stitch over the straight stitches, using one strand of Madeira Red Lacquer 0402. Edge the satin stitch with a tiny running stitch in Madeira Palace Brown 2113.

Bud

Couch the bud in the same manner as the flower, using Cou Copper 371 with Madeira Emperor's Lime 1580 as the sewing thread. Changing the colour of the sewing thread slightly changes the overall colour, making the bud a little greener than the flower.

Stem and leaf

Work the outsides of the stems in running stitch in one strand of Dynasty Green 1540.

Stem outline: The same amount of thread above as below the organza

Fill the stems in running stitch, half in one strand of Emperor's Lime 1580 and half in one strand of Dynasty Green 1540.

Stem filling: More thread below the organza than above.

Work the lower section of the leaf in double-spaced running stitch in one strand of Emperor's Lime 1580, more thread below than above. Work the same running stitch on the top half of the leaf in one strand of Dynasty Green 1540.

**Background
embroidery**

Using one strand of Rajmahal TMTA Light Copper, work waves of
running stitch surrounding the flower.

Background

The embroidery is mounted over a standard stage 5 ½ in (13 cm)
square.

Rose Cottage

This design is influenced by a style of bookplate popular in the early 1900s. The artist would engrave a rural or landscape scene and enclose it with a border of botanical significance to the area. The cottage is embroidered in silk thread on a linen fabric background, the botanical surround embroidered on a layer of organza in the foreground.

The style of embroidery has been chosen to represent the period. The foreground is very traditional, mainly satin stitch, and to a degree overworked. Bordering the design is a circle of two rows of gold cord. The two panels come together, a cloudy cottage scene surrounded by embroidered roses.

Requirements

2 frames 12 ½ in (32 cm) square
organza to cover one frame
⅛ in (3 mm) foam core for background
Madeira 019: Gainsborough Green 1503
Madeira 018: Dusty Rose 0303, Deep Rose 0302, Old Gold 2114, Country Cream 2207, French Yellow 2211
Butterfly Metallic: Antique Gold
sheet of iron-on transfer paper, e.g. Hewlett-Packard C6065A®
cream embroidery linen, approximately 15 in (40 cm) square
mixed embroidery threads (see page 53)

Stitches

Satin stitch, shadow stitch, running stitch, pistil stitch; bullion knots and French knots also used on background embroidery

Transferring the design

Make two frames 12 ½ inches (32 cm) square. Stretch organza onto one frame as detailed on page 21.

Transfer the design onto the framed organza. Centre the frame, organza side down, onto the pattern and trace with a soft black lead pencil or water-erasable pen (see page 21).

Tracing outline (same size)

The philosophy of colouring

Where you are working with various shades of colour in the one flower, as here, it is important to choose colours that will blend into each other. In general, you need three values—a light, a medium and a dark shade. The flowers in this design come in two colourways, pink and yellow, and share the same rather neutral colour for the lightest value.

	Pink colourway	**Yellow colourway**
Light	Country Cream 2207	Country Cream 2207
Medium	Dusty Rose 0303	French Yellow 2211
Dark	Deep Rose 0304	Old Gold 2114

Look at each petal and determine whether it is light, medium or dark
> *Very light*: use only the light value.
> *Light*: start with the medium value and highlight it.
> *Medium*: start with the medium value and add highlight and shadow.
> *Dark*: start with the medium value and add shadow.
> *Very dark*: start with the dark value and highlight with medium value.

Roses

I suggest you refer to the notes on satin stitch on page 17 before you begin embroidering these roses.

Work the medium colours first. Using one strand of Madeira Dusty Rose 0303, loosely satin-stitch all the pink flowers; using one strand of Madeira French Yellow 2211 loosely satin-stitch all the yellow flowers.

Using one strand of Madeira Country Cream 2211, add the highlights to both pink and yellow flowers.

With one strand of Madeira Deep Rose 0304, add the shading to all the pink flowers.

With one strand of Madeira Old Gold 2114, add the shading to all the yellow flowers. Where areas begin to blend, it will be necessary to define them with a split stitch of either the highlight or the shading colour.

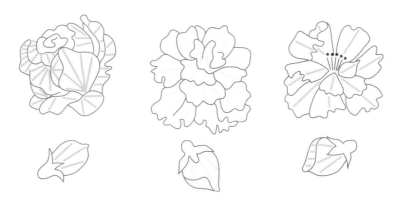

Leaves

Using one strand of Madeira Gainsborough Green 1503, work the six large leaves and three large leaflets at the top of the design in shadow stitch, referring to the photograph and to page 16 for guidance.

Circular border

Using one strand of Butterfly Metallic Antique Gold, work running stitch to create the two circles for the gold border.

Finishing touches

Add shading between the flowers in one strand of Madeira Old Gold 2114, following the photograph for guidance.

Work a few pistil-stitch stamens in one strand of Madeira French Yellow 2211 in the centre of the pink flower. The small leaflets are worked in satin stitch in Madeira Gainsborough Green 1503 on running-stitch stems in the same thread.

The bases of the three buds are worked in one strand of Madeira Gainsborough Green 1503 in straight stitch.

Background

The linen background features a cottage that looks as though it has been painted in watercolours before being lightly embroidered. Scan the coloured picture of the cottage. Print it out onto the iron-on transfer paper, following the manufacturer's instructions.

Cut the transfer down to fit a 4 ¾ inch (12 cm) diameter circle, then, following the manufacturer's instructions, iron the transfer onto a piece of embroidery linen or similar natural fabric—do not use a synthetic fabric here.

(If you do not have the facilities to scan the colour picture, trace the outline diagram of the cottage instead, and wash in the colours on the linen in fabric paints.)

Embroider the garden around the cottage, using stitches such as satin stitch, French knots, bullion, straight stitch.

Because the cottage and its garden will be seen through the screen of the white organza, you need to use brighter colours than usual. I suggest a selection of Madeira silk 018: pinks 0703, 0701, 0210; greens 1602, 1407, 1311; yellows 2211, 0105, 0204; blues 1005, 1102, 1103; purples 0903, 0713, 0803.

Colour picture of cottage has been reversed to come out the right way on the fabric

Assembly

Mount the linen embroidery onto a piece of foam core cut the size of the work frame. Tape the mounted work to the back frame. Bring the framed foreground and background together and join with tape.

**Tracing outline of cottage
for fabric painting**

Trees and bushes:
made up of straight
stitches

Add a few simple
straight stitches to make
highlights on the
cottage—around the
windows, the tops of the
chimneys and along the
top of the roof.

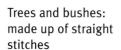

Small flowers:
clusters of colonial
knots and French
knots of varying size.
Bullion stitch is ideal
for flowers such as
lupins.

Lavender: grey straight
stitch for the stems.
Smaller straight stitch in
lavender for the flowers.

Blackberries

Not the friendliest of fruits … I always pictured blackberries when I read Brer Rabbit stories, seeing them as a good refuge for the rabbit and the other small animals. As children we would collect the fruits and think very little of their beauty— other than their taste.

Now is the chance to look at the beauty of the blackberry in terms of shape, texture and colour. In this design we have a combination of textures, ranging from the fine transparency of the leaves to the density of the built-up thread that forms the berries. The design is enhanced by the use of Gumnut Yarns variegated silk thread. The two green threads used here blend beautifully without effort, the variegations leading from one thread to the next. Jumping to the other side of the colour spectrum, Nature adds a deep maroon-red to enhance the greens.

Requirements

2 frames 12 ½ in (32 cm) square
organza to cover one frame
⅛ in (3 mm) white foam core for background and stage
Gumnut Yarns Star: Winter Sky 275, Ripe Berry 299, Briar 547, Hedgerow 587
Madeira 017: Black Bird 514
Madeira 018: Winter Green 705
chicken wire

Stitches

Running stitch, French knots, straight stitch

Transferring
the design

Make two frames 12 ½ inches (32 cm) square. Stretch organza
onto one frame as detailed on page 21.

Transfer the design onto the framed organza. Centre the frame,
organza side down, onto the pattern and trace with a soft black
lead pencil or water-erasable pen (see page 21).

Leaves

Using one strand of Gumnut Yarns Ripe Berry 299, work the
outlines and the ribs of the five leaves in long and short tacking
stitch.

Tracing outline (same size)

Using one strand of Gumnut Yarns Briar 547, loosely work double-spaced long and short tacking stitch between the ribs.

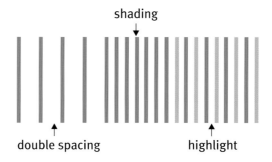

Using one strand of Gumnut Yarns Briar 547, shade the dark areas of leaves 1, 2 and 3.

Using one strand of Gumnut Yards Hedgerow 587, highlight the light areas of leaves 1, 2 and 3.

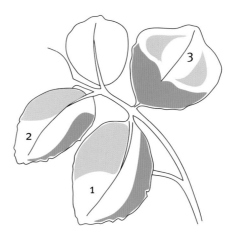

Leave leaf number 4 without shading or highlights.

Using one strand of Gumnut Yarns Briar 547, triple-space lines of long and short tacking stitch between the ribs, according to the numbers on the diagram.

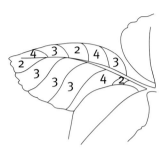

Using one strand of Gumnut Yarns Hedgerow 587, finish leaf 5 by zigzagging between the dark green stitching.

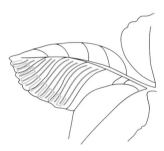

Stems and midveins

Using one strand of Gumnut Yarns Ripe Berry 299, work the stems in running top stitch (refer to page 14).

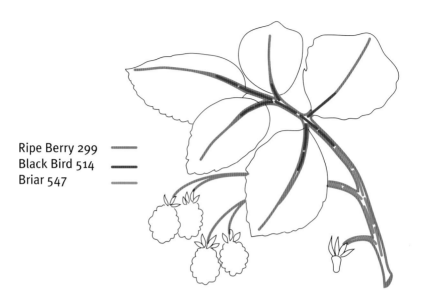

Ripe Berry 299
Black Bird 514
Briar 547

Using one strand of Madeira Black Bird 514, highlight the midvein of each of the leaves.

Finish the leaves by working small straight stitches at the base of each leaf stem in one strand of Gumnut Yarns Briar 547.

Berries

Using six strands of Madeira Black Bird 514, work 5-wrap French knots to form the fruit. Work the two full berries first.

With one strand of Gumnut Yarns Winter Sky 275, straight-stitch over the knots individually on the light sides of the two berries.

With one strand of Gumnut Yarns Ripe Berry 299, stitch over the knots individually on the shade sides of the two berries.

Work the second berry on each stem in 5-wrap French knots in six strands of Madeira Black Bird 514. These two berries are not highlighted or shaded.

Using one strand of Gumnut Yarns Winter Sky 275, work the berry core at lower right in satin stitch.

Using one strand of Gumnut Yarns Briar 547, work the little 'leaves' at the top of each of the four berries and the berry core.

Finishing

Using one strand of Madeira Winter Green 705, and guided by the photograph, work satin stitch of varying densities to create more depth between the leaves. To add interest, create a little hooked tendril with a tiny running stitch.

Background

With this background I have decorated a basic stage with a square of chicken wire slightly larger than the stage so that the wire casts a shadow on the background. Be careful not to snag the organza with the wire.

Beaded Passionfruit

U sing waste canvas as a base allows you to work beading and cross-stitch on organza. I have worked this project using strongly coloured beads in the top section and a form of cross-stitch in the lower section, using several stitches in the one colour to create a lacy look. Two graphs are provided, one in colour for the beading, the other in black and white for the lacework. Regardless of which graph you are using, the top represents the beadwork, the bottom the lacework, which is worked in the same thread used to attach the beads. The beading diagram also gives you the bottom half of the pattern to follow if you wish to bead the whole area.

Requirements

2 frames 12 ½ in (32 cm) square
organza to cover one frame
⅛ in (3 mm) white foam core for background and stage
Delica beads: DBR 12 Raspberry, 35 Galvanised Silver, 201 White Pearl, 352 Matte Cream, 371 Matte Metallic Olive Green, 412 Galvanised Yellow, 456 Galvanised Olive, 657 S/mat s/lined LHT Grey Green
beading thread: 80 m of fine white (used for both beading and embroidery)
waste canvas, 14 count, 12 ½ inches (32 cm) square

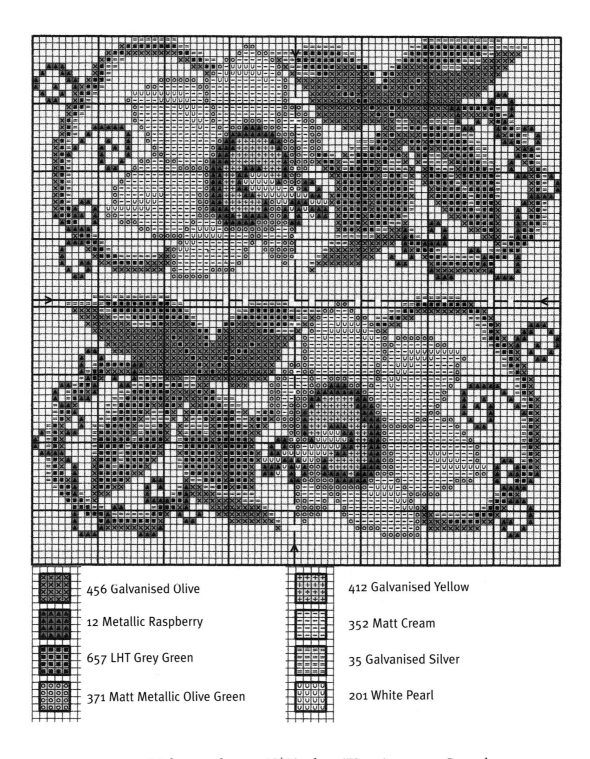

▨ 456 Galvanised Olive		⊞ 412 Galvanised Yellow	
▲ 12 Metallic Raspberry		⊟ 352 Matt Cream	
▦ 657 LHT Grey Green		▤ 35 Galvanised Silver	
◉ 371 Matt Metallic Olive Green		⊍ 201 White Pearl	

Setting up the frames

Make two frames 12½ inches (32 cm) square. Stretch organza onto one frame as detailed on page 21.

Cut a piece of waste canvas the size of the frame. If the canvas is not square, spray lightly with starch and pull into shape. Fasten the canvas with tape to the back of the framed organza.

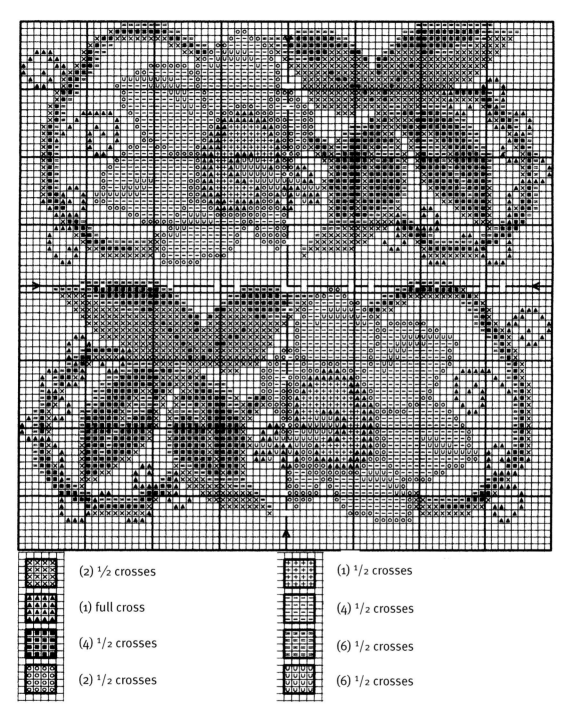

(2) ½ crosses

(1) full cross

(4) ¹/₂ crosses

(2) ¹/₂ crosses

(1) ¹/₂ crosses

(4) ¹/₂ crosses

(6) ¹/₂ crosses

(6) ¹/₂ crosses

(=) the number within brackets means the number of ¹/₂ crosses per stitch

Find both the horizontal and vertical centres and mark them with running stitch in a bright-coloured thread.

Beading

The top half of the diagram is the beaded section. The flowers, leaves, stems and tendrils are all worked in beads. The background is a half cross-stitch worked in the beading thread.

Starting from the top left-hand side of the frame, follow the graph to bead the design. Make a small knot to begin. Where there are no beads, fill the space with a half cross-stitch, or several if you feel they are needed.

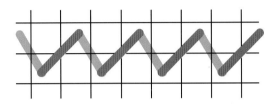

Where a bead is needed, come up through the canvas at A, thread a bead, and go down at B.

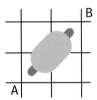

To return right to left, work in reverse—up at B, thread the bead, and go down at A.

Lacework

A lacy look is achieved when using thread only to work the design. Instead of using colour to define the pattern, it is defined here by the number of half cross-stitches worked on top of each other. For example, a Galvanised Silver bead in the top half is replaced by six half cross-stitches in the beading thread (that is, instead of working one half cross and moving on to the next square, you work over that square six times before you move on).

Work the same way as the beaded section, from right to left—up at A and down at B, and on the return, up at B and down at A.

Removing the waste canvas

After the stitching is completed, dampen the waste canvas from the back; do not soak it, as the release lubricant might be washed out. While damp, begin to remove the canvas thread by thread. It will be quite difficult to begin with, and a pair of pliers or tweezers might be handy. It gets easier as you go along. Allow to dry.

Background

Use a basic stage painted a dark colour so that it shows up the white thread. Make the stage a little smaller than the embroidered area; this will give the appearance of squaring up the work as the white stitchery that overlaps the stage will fade into the background.

Agapanthus

The wonderful agapanthus, that harbinger of summer, now comes in many sizes, the flowerhead of the larger varieties truly a bouquet in itself. They also look beautiful after flowering, with a head of seedpods atop the flower stem going a thin, papery light grey. This design shows up the beauty of the variegated Gumnut yarns, giving each petal delicate shadings. The flowers are worked primarily in simple straight satin stitches, either on the surface or under the organza. The leaves are worked in running stitch in two shades of variegated green.

Requirements

2 frames 12 ½ in (32 cm) square
organza to cover one frame
⅛ in (3 mm) white foam core for background and stage
Gumnut Star Silk: Sky Blue 386, Night Blue 388, Mist Green 584,
Native Grass 587
Madeira Silk 018: ecru
dry stem (found object)

Stitches

Running stitch, satin stitch, French knot

**Transferring
the design**

Make two frames 12½ inches (32 cm) square. Stretch organza onto one frame as detailed on page 21.

    Transfer the design onto the framed organza. Centre the frame, organza side down, onto the pattern and trace with a soft black lead pencil or water-erasable pen (see page 21).

    Because of the tightness of the stretched organza it is possible to work long straight stitches side by side without them becoming unmanageable. This design takes full advantage of this quality and travels in long straight stitches above and below the surface (refer to page 73).

**Tracing outline
(same size)**

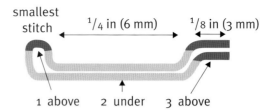

smallest
stitch   ¹/₄ in (6 mm)   ¹/₈ in (3 mm)

1 above   2 under   3 above

Flowers

The petals are worked in a combination satin stitch, partly above the surface and partly below it, as the diagram shows. To begin, bring your thread up at the centre of the flower and work running stitch to the tip of a petal. Following the diagram to work a shadow running stitch: the first stitch needs to be approximately ⅛ in (3 mm) long on the surface of the organza. Travel the thread approximately ¼ in (6 mm) under the organza, come up and take the smallest possible stitch. Go back under the organza, reversing the process.

A

B

C

Using one strand of Gumnut Sky Blue 386 (A) and Gumnut Night Blue 388 (B), work the flowers in running stitch following the diagram. The area C is where the thread is underneath the fabric.

Using one strand of Madeira ecru, work a ring of French knots as stamens, following the photograph for guidance.

Work pinwheels of straight stitch in Gumnut Night Blue 388 for the two circles.

Leaves and stem

Using one strand of Gumnut Native Grass 587 (A) and Gumnut Mist Green 584 (B), work the leaves in a running stitch, following the diagram.

More thread above the organza than below

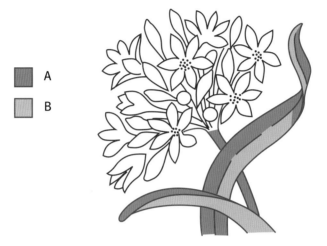

A

B

Work the main stem in running top stitch in Gumnut Native Grass 587, blending into the individual flower stems worked in running top stitch in Gumnut Night Blue 388.

Background

For the background use a simple stage with the lower right-hand corner cut off on the diagonal. Position the cut-off dropped down from the main stage as shown in the photograph, with a smaller triangle glued into the corner to form a ledge for the piece of dried stem. Glue the stem parallel to the diagonals of the triangles.

The Lovely Wren

Wrens, here one moment and gone the next. Always in a hurry, with somewhere else to go, they stop momentarily to give us the pleasure of a glimpse and then they're gone. There are many different species, found in every State of Australia. This one is the Lovely Wren, found in Queensland, the Northern Territory and Western Australia. It is worked predominantly in straight stitch and satin stitch, using several different textures and weights of thread. This form of embroidery suits the subject as it is light, delicate, with a sense that it was applied quickly, just as the glimpse of the bird was a fleeting one.

Requirements

3 frames 12 ½ in (32 cm) square

organza to cover two frames

⅛ in (3 mm) white foam core for background and stage

Madeira 019: Sydney Harbour 1533, Fremantle Blue 1566

Madeira 018: Franklin River 1508, Kakadu 2113, Simpson Desert 2210, Blue Mountains 1008, Kosciusko White, ecru

Gumnut Star: Melbourne Sky 299

Golden Threads Cou: Peacock Blue 341

Madeira 40: Gold 7

Stitches

Satin stitch, straight stitch, colonial knot, running stitch, split stitch

Transferring the design

Make three frames 12 ½ inches (32 cm) square. Stretch organza onto two frames as detailed on page 21.

Transfer the bird design and the background design onto the framed organza. Centre the frames, organza side down, onto the patterns and trace with a soft black lead pencil or water-erasable pen (see page 21).

Tracing outline (same size)

Tracing outline (same size)

Head

The head is the most important part of this design as it reveals the character of the bird and a sense of life; the rest of the body can be more stylised. Using one strand of Madeira Blue Mountains 1008, work a 4-wrap French knot for the eye. Surround the knot with a split-stitch line in the same thread. Using one strand of white cotton or silk, fill in the lower half of the eye.

Using one strand of Madeira Sydney Harbour 1533, work a running stitch teardrop around the eye.

More thread above the organza than below

Using one strand of Madeira Sydney Harbour 1533, work the hood in satin stitch. Using one strand of Madeira Fremantle Blue 1566, blend the darker thread into the bottom of the hood.

Chest

Using one strand of Gumnut Melbourne Sky 299, work the chest in a satin-style running stitch on top of the fabric at the head of the bird, changing two-thirds of the way down into an open running stitch under the fabric. Work the back of the neck in the same manner.

Combination of more thread above than below,
and more thread below than above

Wings

Using one strand of Madeira Sydney Harbour 1533, work an open satin stitch in the upper portion of the wing. Using one strand of Peacock Blue Cou 341, work more satin stitch between the first stitches. Work a little of the same stitch in the right-hand corner of the wing in Fremantle Blue 1566.

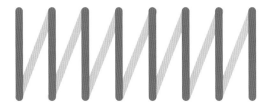

In the second section of the wing, using one strand of Madeira Kakadu 2113, work open satin stitch as before. Using one strand of Madeira Simpson Desert 2210, fill in between the longer stitches with smaller stitches.

In the third section of the wing, using one strand of Gumnut Yarns Melbourne Sky 299, work open satin stitch as before. With one strand of Madeira Blue Mountains 1008, loosely fill in between the stitches to add shading to the top edge of the wing.

Then, using one strand of Madeira Simpson Desert 2210, work some very open long stitches over the two upper sections of the wing.

On the front edge of the wing, using one strand of Madeira Simpson Desert 2210, work four straight stitches couched in the centre to slightly curve them. Begin at the tip of the upper section of the wing, moving down to the third section.

Tail

With one strand of Gumnut Yarns Melbourne Sky 299, fan open long straight stitches the length of the tail. With the same thread fill in the end of the tail to add more colour, varying the length of the stitches so as not to form a straight line, using the photograph as a guide.

Using one strand of Madeira Fremantle Blue 1566, squeeze some small straight stitches into the base of the tail, again varying the length of the stitches.

Legs

Using one strand of Madeira Blue Mountains 1008, work four long stitches from the foot to the body. Couch the stitches together at the knee and the ankle. Work the feet in small straight stitches, satin stitch over the smaller stitches.

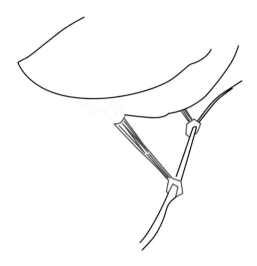

Belly

Using one strand of Madeira Kosciusko White, work the fluffy feathers below the tail with random colonial pistil stitch.

In the same thread, use a running top stitch to outline the underbelly. It is not filled in.

Twig and leaves

Work the twig in running stitch, using one strand of Madeira Franklin River 1508.

More thread above the organza than below

Work the leaves in satin stitch in one strand of Madeira Franklin River 1508.

Background leaf spray

On the second organza-filled frame, work the background design of twigs and leaves in Madeira Franklin River 1508 in the same manner as the foreground twigs and leaves.

Work the butterfly in Madeira 40 Gold 7, using loose lazy daisy stitches for the wings and three straight stitches for the body. The head is a colonial knot and the antennae are worked in straight stitches.

Assembly

Firmly tape the three work frames together before taking the finished embroidery to the framer.

Japanese Plum Blossom

Blossom and fine embroidery are always reminiscent of Japan. The Japanese have made depicting blossom in embroidery not only into an art, but its symbolism has become part of their culture. The plum blossom symbolises new hope, as it flowers in the snow, and because old, tired-looking trees still bear fresh new flowers, it also stands for longevity. To learn the Japanese discipline of fine embroidery takes much time and schooling; please accept this design as my version of an admirable art.

This design is minimal and worked off centre for impact. It has been embroidered in very traditional European-style stitchery in a variety of thread thicknesses, predominantly in satin stitch.

Requirements

2 frames 12 ½ in (32 cm) square
organza to cover one frame
⅛ in (3 mm) white foam core for background and stage
Madeira Silk 018: Kimono Pink 0504, Geisha Blush 0813, Bonsai Brown 2113, Painted Face Ecru
Madeira Cotton 017: Black Plum 2607
Au Ver à Soie perlée: Spring Green 658
colour photocopy of watercolour picture on page 90

Stitches

Long stitch, satin stitch, straight stitch

**Transferring
the design**

Make two frames 12 ½ inches (32 cm) square. Stretch organza
onto one frame as detailed on page 21.

　　Transfer the design onto the framed organza. Centre the frame,
organza side down, onto the pattern and trace with a soft black
lead pencil or water-erasable pen (see page 21).

Tracing outline (same size)

Full-face flower Using one strand of Madeira Painted Face Ecru, fan out long straight stitches, double spaced.

Using the same thread, follow the same fanning, filling in the double space where highlights are needed. Go down into the previous stitch as far as the needle can comfortably go without splitting or overlapping the thread.

With one strand of Madeira Geisha Blush 0813, follow the fan, filling in the double space in the shaded areas on the outer parts of the petals.

With one strand of Madeira Kimono Pink, follow the fanning, and fill in from the centre of the flower, working out where heavy shading is needed.

Having established the basics, add to the highlights and shading, still keeping the fanning, using the photograph as a guide.

Finish the flower by adding stamens in straight stitch in Madeira Black Plum 2607.

Profile flower   Follow the same principles to work the petals of the profile flower.

**Buds and
flower base**

Using one strand of Au Ver à Soie perlée Spring Green 658, work the buds and the base of the flower that has lost its petals. Start with a long stitch to the point of each bud, working back with smaller and smaller stitches until the area is covered.

Add straight stitches in Madeira Kimono Pink at the tip of the buds and within the flower base, following the diagram.

Stem

Work a running stitch outline for the stem in one strand of Madeira Bonsai Brown 2113. Give more weight to the right-hand side, around the buds. Add a little brown amongst the green at the bases of the buds.

More thread above the organza than below

Using one strand of Madeira Bonsai Brown 2113, lightly fill in the back of the stem with long straight stitches.

Background   This design has a simple stage background (see page 23), with a colour photocopy of the watercolour picture on this page glued to it.

Make a colour photocopy of this painting at 100%

Passionflower

The passionfruit flower, with its primitive yet exotic look, is always featured in portfolios of botanical art. Its name was given to it by early Spanish friars who saw it as a symbol of the passion of Christ, the five anthers representing the five wounds suffered by Christ, and the triple style representing the three nails, two for the hands and one for the feet. In the receptacle is seen the cross, and in the corona the crown of thorns.

This design uses a variety of threads, from the thickness of Au Ver à Soie perlée to the variegated Gumnut Yarns and the fine YLI silks. Just as the thickness of threads differs in this design so does the depth of the stitching; some areas have detail while other areas have just a hint of colour and form.

Requirements

2 frames 12 ½ in (32 cm) square
organza to cover one frame
⅛ in (3 mm) white foam core for background
Gumnut Star Silk: Glory Yellow 706, Golgotha Green 784,
Gethsemane Green 584
YLI Silk: Righteous White 16, Benediction Wine 818, Justification Rose 822
Au Ver à Soie perlée: Purple Majesty 133, Resurrection Green 659
white 4-sheet cardboard

Stitches

Running stitch, straight stitch, satin stitch

Transferring the design

Make two frames 12 ½ inches (32 cm) square. Stretch organza onto one frame as detailed on page 21.

Transfer the design onto the framed organza. Centre the frame, organza side down, onto the pattern and trace with a soft black lead pencil or water-erasable pen (see page 21).

Tracing outline (same size)

Flower petals

Using one strand of Gumnut Glory Yellow 706, work the outline of the petals in running stitch.

More thread above the organza than below

Starting at the outer edge of the ring of stamens, fill in the petals with running stitch, working with quadruple spacing. (This is because the next thread will be stitched between the Glory Yellow to make double spacing.)

More thread below the organza than above

Work the eight front petals with the quadruple spacing, leaving the two back (topmost) petals more open, with only two or three rows of stitching. The aim here is to start off very light and build up.

Using one strand of YLI Righteous White 16, work a running stitch between the yellow on seven of the front petals; on the eighth petal (on the left), work only half (see photograph). The YLI silk, being fine, will add to the overall lightness.

It is now time to begin to build up the colour and form of the petals to distinguish between them. Using Glory Yellow for depth and Righteous White for the highlight, begin to top stitch the front four petals. Work mainly on the front two, as indicated in the diagram.

Bud

The bud is worked in a slightly different manner, getting its shading from the stitch itself. Outline the bud with a top stitch running stitch in Glory Yellow. Again use quadruple spacing to fill in, this time working the lower part of the bud in the top stitch, and the upper part in the underneath stitch. Fill between the first lines of stitching with the Righteous White but in reverse, using running top stitch for the lower part of the bud, and running bottom stitch for the upper part.

Flower stamens

The stamens are worked in one strand of Au Ver à Soie perlée Benediction Wine 818. Work a zigzag around the outer circle, thickening the front part of the stamens. Next, place a long straight stitch between the head of each stamen and the centre of the circle, leaving a tiny space between head and stem.

Following the diagram, and using one strand of Gumnut Glory Yellow 706, fill in between the stamen stems. Do not cover the stems with the Glory Yellow, but divide the thread, forcing the Glory Yellow between.

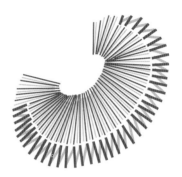

With one strand of YLI Righteous White 16, highlight the Glory Yellow between the front stamens, crossing the thread diagonally across the Glory Yellow.

Pistil

To embroider the pistil, work around the base first in running stitch in one strand of Au Ver à Soie perlée Resurrection Green 659, then couch over the running stitch with a satin stitch in the front.

With one strand of Au Ver à Soie perlée Purple Majesty 133, work four long straight stitches for the pistil itself, couching these together with a stitch about ⅛ in (4 mm) from the base and another the same distance from the top. At the base, fill in around the straight stitches with satin stitch.

Following the photograph as a guide, add the triple style at the top of the pistil, using one strand of Au Ver à Soie perlée Justification Rose 822. Work small stitches for the twig-like part, using satin stitch to make the 'pods' at the ends.

Leaves

Guided by the photograph and the diagram, embroider the upper leaves in one strand of Gumnut Golgotha Green 784 and one strand of Gethsemane Green 584, blending the colours so that the leaves are lighter at the top and become darker towards the bottom.

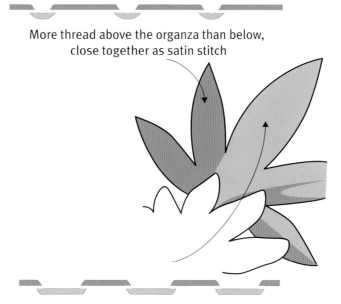

More thread above the organza than below, close together as satin stitch

The same amount of thread above as below the organza, double-spaced stitching

Work the two lower leaves using one strand of Gumnut Gethsemane Green 584. Work leaf A in shadow satin stitch (refer to page 16), beginning with double spacing and closing up into satin stitch. Over the top of the shadow satin stitch work some long straight stitches. Work leaf B in double-spaced shadow satin stitch.

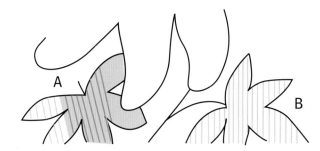

Bud calyx

With one strand of Gumnut Gethsemane Green 584, work the bud calyx in satin stitch, adding a satin-stitch covered knot at the base.

Stems

Using one strand of YLI Benediction Wine 818, work the stems in three rows of running stitch, the tendrils in one row. Then couch the stems in Gumnut Gethsemane Green 584, working heavily at the bottom and decreasing the intensity as you get to the top. Embroider the leaves as you work up the stem in five straight stitches of varying lengths.

Background

Trace the pattern again onto a sheet of tracing paper. Place the tracing face up on a piece of white 4-sheet card 9 in (23 cm) square. With a sharp craft knife cut around the outline of the tracing, leaving small bridges uncut to keep the design from falling apart. Invert the card (see photograph for the required effect) and gently push up the edges of the cuts to create shadows. Glue the card to the foam core background with dry glue (glue stick).

Sweet Peas

For me the sweet pea is a 'Grandmother' flower—when it decorates old bone china, wallpapers, chintz, talcum powder containers—and yet it is also used in simple, modern bridal bouquets. Although the sweet pea was often depicted in bright colours, it was also used as a pattern for lace and damask. This design reflects that side of the flower, using soft colours and textures.

This project is rather different in that it is worked in soft cotton rather than silk. The aim here is to create a contrast between the sheer and delicate organza and the thick, natural cotton candlewicking thread that is more often used for work on raw fabrics like seeded homespun. The colonial knot brings a pin-spot lace feel to the background.

Requirements

2 frames 12 ½ in (32 cm) square

organza to cover one frame

⅛ in (3 mm) white foam core for background and stage

2-ply loose twist Traditional Candlewicking Thread (available through Gary Clarke Designs, see suppliers list): Bridesmaid Pink, Page Boy Green, Bridal Veil

Stitches

Satin stitch, colonial knot, straight stitch, running stitch, split stitch

Transferring the design

Make two frames 12 ½ inches (32 cm) square. Stretch organza onto one frame as detailed on page 21.

Transfer the design onto the framed organza. Centre the frame, organza side down, onto the pattern and trace with a soft black lead pencil or water-erasable pen (see page 21).

Tracing outline (same size)

Flowers

Using one strand of Bridesmaid Pink cotton, work all flower outlines in split stitch. Split stitch is good here in that it will mould around the sharp curves of the petals; it also gives a good smooth edge to provide a foundation for satin stitch.

Using one strand of Bridesmaid Pink cotton, satin stitch over the split stitch shapes. When shaping satin stitch in directional stitches, lay down a spaced row of stitches first. Then lay down a series of rows to fill in. This will ensure a smooth movement of the thread. When the work becomes too tight to fit another thread alongside, divide the stitches and place a stitch comfortably between. Fan out the stitching as indicated in the diagram.

Stems and leaves

Using one strand of Page Boy Green, work a split stitch for the stems, converting to a small running stitch at the tendrils.

Again using one strand of Page Boy Green, cover the split stitch stems with satin stitch, decreasing towards the tendrils.

Still with one strand of Page Boy Green, embroider the leaves in a series of straight stitches lying side by side as in satin stitch. Work the longest straight stitch first, then stitches decreasing in size to the sides.

Using the same thread, satin-stitch the two flower bases.

Colonial knot background

Using one strand of Bridal Veil and guided by the photograph, work lines of colonial knots around the cluster of flowers, beginning in the centre and working to the outer edge. The thread running between the knots lies under the organza.

Background

Use a simple stage for the background, as described on page 23.

Monkey

For me this monkey conjures up romantic images of a bygone era—the beginnings of the British Empire, oriental traders dealing in silks, gold and precious jewels, crowded bazaars with exotic smells and sounds, interesting characters from many nations. Or perhaps he was an organ-grinder's monkey, entertaining children in the park. Whichever, he is dressed in his best to impress in rich reds and gold.

Requirements

2 frames 12 ½ in (32 cm) square

organza to cover one frame

⅛ in (3 mm) white foam core for background and stage

Madeira 018: Raffles Grey 1910, Rattan 2114, Singapore Sand 2210

YLI Silk: Caftan White 13

Au Ver à Soie perlée: Empire Red 384, Bamboo Green 654, Rickshaw Blue 768

Golden Threads Cou: Ex Gold D371

white 4-sheet cardboard

Stitches

Straight stitch, satin stitch, couching

**Transferring
the design**

Make two frames 12 ½ inches (32 cm) square. Stretch organza onto one frame as detailed on page 21.

Transfer the design onto the framed organza. Centre the frame, organza side down, onto the pattern and trace with a soft black lead pencil or water-erasable pen (see page 21).

Tracing outline (same size)

Face

On any design of this nature I like to work the face first; this way one gets a feeling for the personality of the person or animal.

Remember, when you are moulding satin stitch, begin with open stitches as shown in the diagram to determine stitch direction, then fill between them.

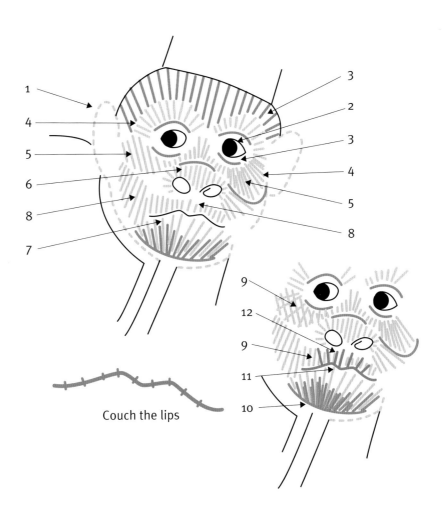

Couch the lips

The numbered steps below relate to the numbers on the diagram.

1. Using one strand of Madeira Singapore Sand 2210, shadow satin stitch the face of the monkey (refer to page 16).
2. Using one strand of Madeira Black, satin-stitch the eyes.
3. Using one strand Madeira Rattan 2114, work satin stitch around the head of the monkey for the 'hair', and couch above and below the eyes.
4. Using one strand Madeira Raffles Grey 1910, satin stitch around the eyes and left cheek.

5. Using one strand of Madeira Singapore Sand 2210, satin stitch the bridge of the nose and right cheek, and shade the left.

6. Using one strand of Madeira Raffles Grey 1910, satin stitch the nose of the monkey.

7. Using one strand of Madeira Singapore Sand 2210, satin stitch the chin.

8. Using one strand of Madeira Singapore Sand 2210, satin stitch under the cheeks and around the top lip.

9. Using one strand of YLI Caftan White 13, work open fanned satin stitch over the right cheek, under the eye. Using the same thread, work a series of straight stitches over the lip.

10. Using one strand of Madeira Raffles Grey 1910, fan a light satin stitch under the chin for shading.

11. Using one strand of Madeira Raffles Grey 1910, highlight the bottom lip.

12. Using one strand of Madeira Black, define the mouth, nose shape and the shadow under the chin.

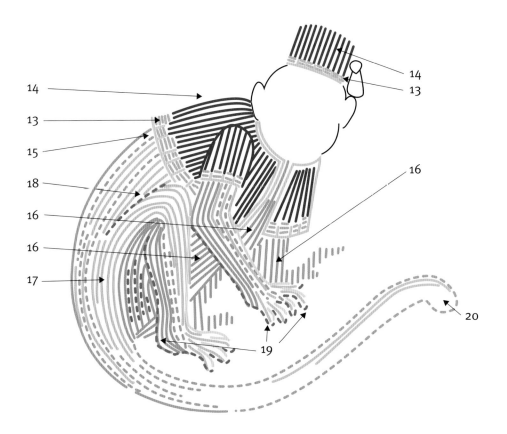

Body

13. Using one strand of Au Ver à Soie perlée Rickshaw Blue 768, trim the fez and jacket in satin stitch.
14. Using one strand of Au Ver à Soie perlée Empire Red 384, satin-stitch the fez and jacket.
15. Using Cou Ex Gold D 371, couch a trim around the fez and jacket, using a gold sewing machine thread to couch down the cord.
16. Using one strand of Madeira Rattan 2114, satin-stitch the chest and outer arm and leg.
17. Using one strand of Madeira Rattan 2114 and Singapore Sand 2210, work the body in a long and short stitch. Use the diagram to assist in blending the colours. Shape the stitches as shown.
18. Using one strand of Madeira Raffles Grey 1910, highlight the front leg and arm. Use one strand of Madeira Black to shade the back of the arm and leg.
19. Using one strand of Madeira Raffles Grey 1910 and Black, define the feet and hands.
20. Using one strand of Madeira Rattan 2114 and Singapore Sand 2210, work the tail with running long and short stitch (refer to page 15). Keep stitching to a minimum to enhance the transparency of the fabric.
21. Using one strand of Au Ver à Soie perlée Bamboo Green 654, work the branch with running long and short stitch (refer to page 15).

Tassels

Using the three Au Ver à Soie perlée colours, make two tassels, one for the fez, the other for the back of the jacket.

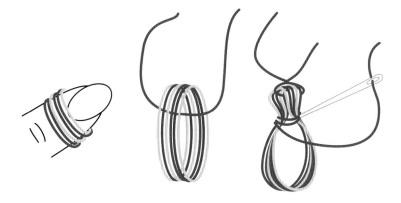

A

B

Tracing patterns for background

Wrap the threads around the tip of your index finger; the more wraps, the fatter the tassel.

Pass a piece of thread through the hank of thread and tie firmly.

Wrap a thread with needle attached around the hank and stitch to secure. Pass the needle through the centre of the hank and remove the needle.

Finish by trimming the ends.

Background

The stage for this design follows the principle of the basic foam core stage, but is made of cut-out 4-sheet card with pieces of foam core glued behind.

Trace the background patterns onto tracing paper. Place each tracing face up on a piece of white card. With a sharp craft knife cut around the outline of the tracing, and cut out the leaves and along the narrow stem areas.

Piece A is cut from a 5 ½ in (13 cm) square of 4-sheet card the size of a stage. The shaded areas represent pieces of foam core glued to the back to hold the card above the background.

Piece B is cut from another 5 ½ in (13 cm) square of 4-sheet card. Glue small pieces of foam core to the underside in the positions indicated by the shaded areas, then glue piece B on top of piece A. (That is, B is raised up from A, A is raised up from the background.)

The monkey and the cut-out sections cast interesting shadows on the background.

Indian Elephant

The Indian elephant is an ancient animal from an ancient land of mystique and grandeur, a land of ornate designs of silver, gold and jewels. This elephant is both richly decorated and part of the decoration.

This is the sort of design that is hard to spoil by overworking, so feel free to keep adding to the embellishment. You might like to add a piece or two of jewellery—perhaps that one earring that you just couldn't throw away. I have used a lot of YLI silk in the embroidery, the smooth fine thread giving an almost watercolour effect.

Requirements

2 frames 12 ½ in (32 cm) square

organza to cover one frame

⅛ in (3 mm) white foam core for background and stage

YLI Silk: Turkish Delight 22, Ancient Stone 46, Indian Lime 114, Taj Mahal 798, Pomegranate 822

Madeira 9844/30: 6032 Gold (machine thread)

Madeira Silk 018: Colonial Grey 1714

Benson & Johnson: Ex Gold 371

Benson & Johnson Cou: Cedar Green 371

Delica beads: DBR Mat Metallic White Gold 336

Mill Hill Crystal Treasures: Teardrop 13052, Heart 13037

white 4-sheet cardboard

Stitches

Running stitch, straight stitch, couching

**Transferring
the design**

Make two frames 12 ½ inches (32 cm) square. Stretch organza
onto one frame as detailed on page 21.

Transfer the design onto the framed organza. Centre the frame,
organza side down, onto the pattern and trace with a soft black
lead pencil or water-erasable pen (see page 21).

In working this rather elaborate design you will probably need
to refer to the photograph quite frequently, particularly when
embroidering the canopy of the howdah, and the saddle blanket.

Tracing outline (same size)

Body

Using one strand of Madeira Colonial Grey 1714, work around the outline of the elephant, including ears and mouth, in a running stitch.

More thread above the organza than below

Using one strand of YLI Ancient Stone 46, fill in the body in a fanned straight stitch, and work the ears with a light running stitch. Work knee and toenails in satin stitch. Be guided by the photograph.

Eye

Work the elephant's eye using one strand of Madeira Colonial Grey 1714—satin stitch for the pupil and couched straight stitches for the surrounds.

Hat

Using one strand of YLI Turkish Delight 22 and one strand of Madeira Gold, work the main part of the elephant's hat in lines of running stitch radiating from the top.

Using 2 strands of Madeira Gold, work a satin-stitch dot at the top, finished with a straight stitch for a 'finial'.
Using one strand of YLI Ancient Stone 46, stitch down a row of Delica beads 336 around the bottom edge of the hat. Link the beads with 2 strands of Madeira Gold machine thread.

With 2 strands of Madeira Gold machine thread, make loops for the cords draping below the line of beads. Couch down the loops, anchoring them with one strand of the same thread.

Howdah

Couch the canopy of the howdah in one strand of Cedar Green Cou. Following the diagram, and referring to the photograph for extra guidance, start at the point indicated by the arrow in the diagram, move over the top, then begin to fill in with gentle curves. When filling in, work to the top, then close alongside the previous couching until ready to go down, zigzagging up and down until a latticework is formed.

Work a cross-stitch in one strand of YLI Turkish Delight 22 at each junction of the lattice.

Stitch a Delica bead in each gap in the lattice, using one strand of YLI Ancient Stone 46. Take the thread along the back of the organza from bead to bead.

Using 2 strands of Madeira Gold, work a satin stitch for the three areas of fretwork at the base of the canopy. Below that sew a row of Delica beads, alternating them vertically and sideways (see diagram).

Under the beads couch two lines of Cedar Green Cou cord.

Two make the curtains, work alternate lines of running stitch in one strand of YLI Turkish Delight 22 and one strand of Madeira Gold.

The same amount of thread above as below the organza

With 2 strands of Madeira Gold, lay three long straight horizontal stitches for the railings of the howdah. Next, work seven verticals in the same manner over the top of the horizontals. Finish off by couching at each point where the threads intersect.

Saddle blanket

Couch around the outline of the blanket using one strand of Ex Gold Cou. Make a loop at the bottom corners to form the right angles.

Using one strand of YLI Turkish Delight 22, work a running stitch inside the couched gold cord.

Using one strand of YLI Indian Lime 14, work two long straight stitches vertically, about ⅛ in (4 mm) in from the Turkish Delight stitch; do the same horizontally. Cross the horizontal stitches over the vertical stitches.

With one strand at a time of YLI Taj Mahal Blue 798, Turkish Delight 22 and then Pomegranate 822, zigzag each thread in turn around the edge of the blanket between the Turkish Delight and Indian Lime stitching.

Using one strand of YLI Pomegranate 822, work two long straight stitches vertically, about ⅛ in (4 mm) in from the Turkish Delight stitch; do the same horizontally. Cross the horizontal stitches over the vertical stitches.

Now, using one strand of YLI Taj Mahal Blue 798, work two straight stitches along the inside of the YLI Indian Lime 114, stitching both vertically and horizontally. Work a diagonal cross-stitch in the square created by the crossed Turkish Delight stitches.

Using two strands of Madeira Gold, work a row of French knots between the Taj Mahal Blue and Turkish Delight stitches. Place a knot in the middle of the cross-stitch at the corner.

Working with one strand of YLI Taj Mahal Blue 798, fill the centre of the blanket with a loose shadowed satin stitch (refer to page 16).

Embellishments   Attach the crystal heart in the middle of the blanket. Stitch the crystal teardrop, pointed end up, at the top of the canopy.

Using a mixture of all the colours in the blanket, make three tassels, one for each corner of the blanket and one for the front of the hat.

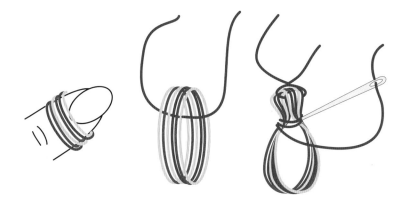

Wrap the threads around the tip of your index finger; the more wraps, the fatter the tassel.

Pass a piece of thread through the hank of thread and tie firmly.

Wrap a thread with needle attached around the hank and stitch to secure. Pass the needle through the centre of the hank and remove the needle.

Finish by trimming the ends.

Background

The stage for this design follows the principle of the basic foam core stage, but is made of cut-out 4-sheet card with pieces of foam core glued behind.

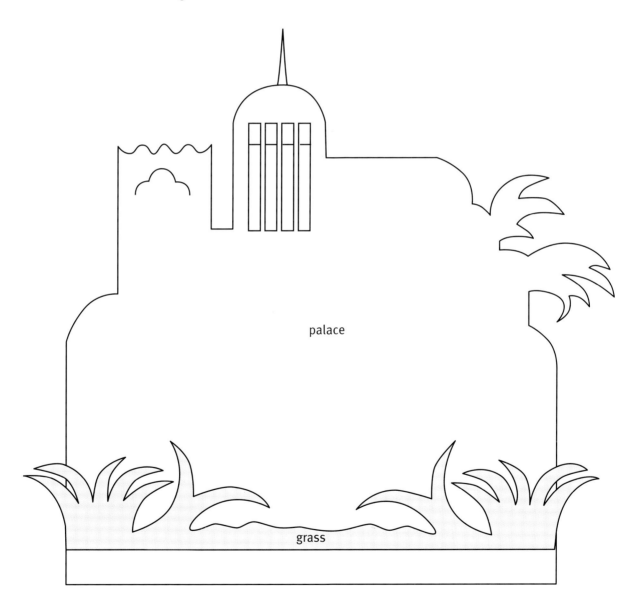

palace

grass

Trace the background patterns for the palace and the grass (shaded section) onto two pieces of tracing paper. Place each tracing face up on a piece of white card. With a sharp craft knife cut around the outlines.

Cut along the line of the curved shape at the top left of the palace, and gently bend it backward.

Cut away the bottom sections of the four narrow windows, then cut along the sides of the top sections and gently bend them forward.

Mount the palace shape to the stage with a horizontal rectangle of foam core. Mount the grass to the foot of the palace shape in the position shown on the tracing pattern, separated by a narrow horizontal strip of foam core

Little Bo-Peep

Many of the nursery rhymes that we know today originated as well-crafted political satire, created in the days before free speech when to speak out against the status quo might have resulted in losing one's head. Today they are romantic reminders of the past.

Our young shepherdess is created with seven simple stitches. The background is a simple sketched outline of her sheep, with a verse of this popular nursery thyme at the bottom.

Requirements

2 rectangular frames, 8 ½ x 14 ½ in (21 x 37 cm)

organza to cover one frame

⅛ in (3 mm) white foam core for background

Madeira Silk 108: Lambs Tail White, Little Boy Blue 1003, Golden Pear Yellow 2208, Dickory Dock Grey 1708, Fiddlers Brown 2113, Pea Green Broth 1408

Madeira 40: Gold 7

4 mm pale blue silk ribbon

colour photocopy of coloured drawing.

Vleisofix®

Stitches

Long stitch, straight stitch, satin stitch, running stitch, running satin stitch, blanket stitch, French knot, damask stitch

Little Bo-peep has lost her sheep,
And can't tell where to find them;
Leave them alone, and they'll come home,
Bringing their tails behind them.

Transferring the design

Make two frames measuring 8 ½ x 14 ½ in (21 x 37 cm). Stretch organza onto one frame as detailed on page 21.

Transfer the design onto the framed organza. Centre the frame, organza side down, onto the pattern and trace the pattern with a soft black lead pencil (do *not* use a water erasable pen, as it will become permanent when the hands and face are ironed into place). Details page 21.

Tracing outline (same size)

Make a photocopy of the partially coloured drawing of Little Bo-Peep. Fuse a small piece of Vleisofix to the printed side. Carefully cut out the face and hands. Place the cut-outs on the back of the organza, using the tracing as a guide, and fuse to the organza, using the backing paper to protect the iron. See page 22 for more information.

Colour photocopy this picture at 100%

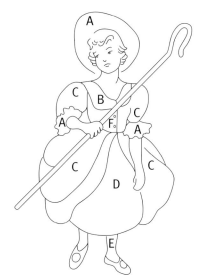

Embroider the design section by section

Dress

A: Using one strand of Madeira Lambs Tail White, fan long straight stitches out around the hat and cuffs in the directions shown in the diagram.

B: Using one strand of Madeira Lambs Tail White, work the collar with long straight stitches.

C: Using one strand of Madeira Little Boy Blue 1003, Golden Pear Yellow 2208, and Lambs Tail White, work consecutive lines of running stitch around the tops of the sleeves and the overskirts of the dress.

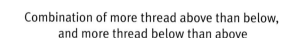

Combination of more thread above than below,
and more thread below than above

D: Using one strand of Madeira Dickory Dock Grey 1708, create a damask look in the centre panel of the skirt through the use of long stitches above and below the organza, like a running stitch. The stitches on the top of the organza will make the pattern of bows and loops. Use the anchoring of the stitch from the top of the fabric to the underneath as an opportunity to slightly curve the overall stitch.

E: Using one strand of Madeira Lambs Tail White for the stockings and Dickory Dock Grey 1708 for the slippers, shape with satin stitch.

F: Using Madeira 40 Gold 7, fill in the bodice of the dress with a close running stitch.

L ittle Bo-Peep has lost her sheep,
And can't tell where to find them;
Leave them alone, and they'll come home,
Bringing their tails behind them.

Embellishments

Edge the hat with a running stitch, and decorate it with a cluster of French knots, using one strand of Madeira Little Boy Blue 1003.

Using one strand of Madeira Lambs Tail White, trim the edges of the collar, first with a running stitch, then working a blanket stitch through the running stitch.

Using one strand of Madeira Little Boy Blue 1003, work 'smocking' across the bodice with three rows of running stitch.

Stitch a star on each slipper using one strand of Madeira 40 Gold 7.

Work five long stitches in one strand of Madeira Fiddlers Brown 2113 along the length of the straight portion of the crook, couching them down randomly with the same thread. Work the bent portion of the crook in five rows of close running stitch.

Using one strand of Madeira Pea Broth Green 1408, work a long running stitch around Little Bo-Peep's feet to give an impression of grass.

Add a silk ribbon bow at the waist and near the bend of the crook.

Background

Photocopy the background design of three sheep and the verse of the nursery rhyme, and dry glue it to the foam core background. (You may prefer to draw the sheep and hand-letter the verse if you have skills in this direction.)

Butterfly

utterflies, light and delicate. My aim with this piece was to create the illusion of lightness so characteristic of a butterfly. It is also an exercise in three-dimensional embroidery, departing somewhat from the conventional in that no wire is used in the wings. My butterfly has gemstones and 2-carat gold bullion embroidered into it. Beads would be just as effective as the gemstones, if not as opulent.

Requirements

2 frames 11 ½ in (29 cm) square
organza to cover one frame, plus extra piece 8 in (20 cm) square
6 in (15 cm) bound hoop
⅛ in (3 mm) white foam core for background and stage
Madeira 018: Californian Poppy 0214, Boronia 0401, Campanula 0801,
Lavender 0803, Cornflower 0902, Green Plum 1409, Ivy Green 1407,
Spring Grass 1603, Flannel Flower 1912, Wattle 2207, Black
Madeira 40: Gold 7
Smooth Purl GILK-5SP (gold bullion)
beading thread
colour photocopy of coloured drawing
Vleisofix®

Stitches

Straight stitch, satin stitch, running stitch, French knots, tufting, blanket stitch laced

Transferring the design

Make two frames 11 ½ inches (29 cm) square. Stretch organza onto one frame as detailed on page 21.

Transfer the maidenhair fern design onto the framed organza. Centre the frame, organza side down, onto the pattern and trace with a soft black lead pencil or water-erasable pen (see page 21). Work the embroidery for the maidenhair fern and the body below and put aside while you work the butterfly's wings.

Tracing outline (same size)

Colour photocopy at 100%

Wings

Make a colour photocopy of the wing design at 100 per cent and fuse the Vleisofix to the printed side. Remove and retain the paper backing. Carefully cut out the wings. Place the wings, printed side up, on a firm ironing surface, approximately ¾ in (2 cm) apart. Centre an 8 in (20 cm) square of organza over the wings, place the backing paper over the organza as an ironing shield, and fuse the organza to the wings.

Fix the square of organza in the embroidery hoop.

Using one strand of Madeira Campanula 0801, work the veins shown in the first section of the diagram in long straight stitches.

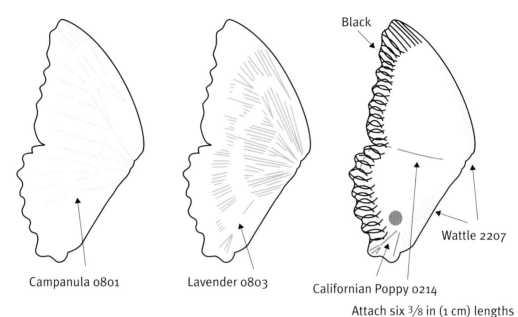

Black

Wattle 2207

Campanula 0801

Lavender 0803

Californian Poppy 0214

Attach six ³⁄₈ in (1 cm) lengths
of gold bullion over the area
embroidered in Wattle 2207

Stitch instructions for wings

With one strand of Madeira Lavender 0803, work straight stitches as indicated in the middle section of the diagram, then work smaller straight stitches in one strand of Madeira Cornflower 0902 between the Lavender stitches.

Following the third section of the diagram, use one strand of Madeira Wattle 2207 to work satin stitch along the front of the wing.

Using one strand of Madeira Wattle 2207, work a cluster of lazy daisies with extended catching stitches at the inside bottom of each wing. Work a straight stitch in the middle of each lazy daisy in one strand of Campanula 0801.

With one strand of Madeira Californian Poppy 0214, work a long straight stitch dividing the front part of the wing from the back part, and continue in a gentle curve in running stitch onto the back part of the wing (see photograph for guidance). Work a satin stitch dot in the same thread on the lower section of the wing, and some small straight stitches in the bottom tip.

Using one strand of Madeira Black, work a small area of satin stitch at the tip of the wing, then work blanket stitch right along the outer edge of the wing.

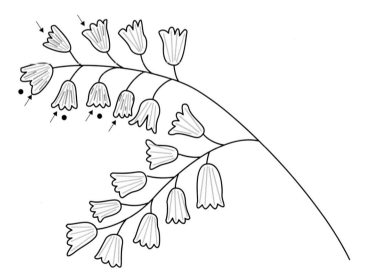

Thread one strand of Madeira Wattle 2207 through the blanket stitch on the front part of the wing, and one strand of Madeira Cornflower 0902 through the blanket stitch on the back part of the wing.

Finish the wing by attaching six ⅜ in (1 cm) pieces of gold bullion (cut with a sharp craft knife) over the Madeira Wattle 2207 at the inner back section of the wing. Treat each piece as a bead, threading a fine needle with beading thread down the centre and attaching at each end.

Use beads to add further lustre to the wings and body.

Repeat for the other wing.

Finally, take the embroidery from the hoop and cut around each wing with very sharp scissors.

Maidenhair fern spray

Work the leaflets in satin stitch in one strand of Madeira Spring Grass 1603.

Highlight the six leaflets indicated in satin stitch in one strand of Madeira Green Plum 1409.

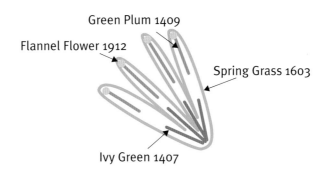

Green Plum 1409

Flannel Flower 1912

Spring Grass 1603

Ivy Green 1407

Using satin stitch in one strand of Madeira Ivy Green 1407, add a little depth of colour at the base of the three leaflets indicated by the external dot.

Work single-wrap French knots, in one strand of Madeira Flannel Flower 1912, at the tips of the same three leaflets.

The stems are worked in running stitch in one strand of Madeira Boronia 0401. Shape and thicken the lower part of the main stem with three lines of running stitch side by side, decreasing to two lines and then one as you move towards the tip of the stem, using the photograph as a guide to the greens used to join the leaflets to the stem, and the way they wrap into the stem.

Body of butterfly

Work the butterfly's body beside the maidenhair fern spray, following the directions in the diagram. Start by cutting five ⅜ in (1 cm) lengths of gold bullion with a very sharp craft knife.

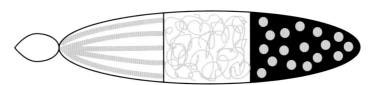

Satin stitch the head in Flannel Flower 1912

Couched gold bullion.
1. Thread the needle with a length of Madeira Gold 7, attaching the five pieces of gold bullion at each end.
2. Couch the bullion into shape.

Tufting
1. Using Madeira Flannel Flower 1912, fill in the area with a series of loops sewn into each other, preventing them from coming undone. Trim the loops when finished.

Padded satin stitch
1. Work long straight stitches in Madeira Black from middle to tip.
2. Satin stitch over the long stitches in the same thread, working from side to side.

3. Work gold French knots in Madeira Gold 7 over the black.

Assembling butterfly

Using Madeira Flannel Flower 1912, attach the left wing to the body with small straight stitches, using a small piece of foam core or cork to hold the wing up from the surface of the organza.

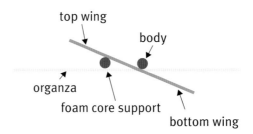

Attach the right wing to the body under the organza, using stitches of the same length and colour.

Attach two small, shiny black beads for the eyes.

Using Madeira 40 Gold 7, create the antennae with long tacking stitches, starting at the body and working out.

Background

Use a plain white foam core background without a stage.

Christmas Tree

The custom of the Christmas tree derives from a pagan ritual, originally practiced at the time of the winter solstice, which gave comfort with its assurance that winter would end and the seemingly dead landscape would again spring to life. Early European Christians, knowing they could not stop the practice, instead gave it new meaning. Based on Isaiah 11:1 they painted a new picture, the branches of the tree symbolising the coming of Christ. The wreath placed on doors during Advent also derives from an earlier custom, when its evergreen branches were thought to protect the home from evil spirits and the holly berries to keep away witches. With Christianity the symbolism changed, the evergreen branches now representing the everlasting life promised by Christ and the round shape representing His crown of thorns.

Requirements

2 frames 12 ½ in (32 cm) square
organza to cover one frame
⅛ in (3 mm) white foam core for background and supports
Golden Threads: Wavy Passing Gilt No. 6
Madeira Heavy Metal Art 9844: 30 6032
Au Ver à Soie Silk: Purple 133, Green 199, Rust 525
white 4-sheet cardboard

Stitches

Couching stitch, running stitch, straight stitch, colonial knot

**Transferring
the design**

Make two frames 12 ½ inches (32 cm) square. Stretch organza
onto one frame as detailed on page 21.

Transfer the tree and wreath design onto the framed organza.
Centre the frame, organza side down, onto the pattern and trace
with a soft black lead pencil or water-erasable pen (see page 21).

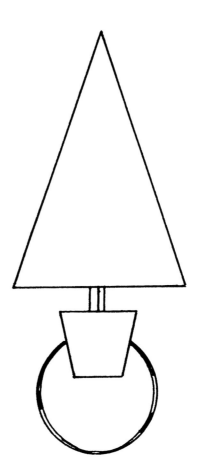

Tracing outline (same size)

Tree

Begin the cone of the tree using one strand of Au Ver à Soie Green 199, working seven long straight stitches coming to a point at the top of the cone.

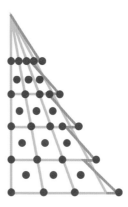

Couch all seven straight stitches with a zigzag stitch in one strand of the same thread. The two outer-edge zigzags must be mirror images of each other.

Using one strand of Au Ver à Soie Purple 133, work colonial knots at regular intervals over the cone. (Be aware that this colour may bleed when wet, as I found out the hard way. It may be wise to leave this section and the trunk until last, if you have used a water-erasable pen to trace the design. If you used pencil, there will be no problem.)

Using a couching stitch, thread the Wavy Passing Gilt between the knots as if placing tinsel on a tree, using ordinary sewing cotton as the sewing thread.

Work the six-pointed star at the top of the tree with Madeira Gold, first with three straight stitches crossing in the centre, then filling in around the edges with straight-stitch triangles.

Work the trunk in Au Ver à Soie Purple 133, using straight stitches on the back of the fabric.

Pot

Using one strand of Au Ver à Soie Rust 525, work the pot in straight stitches, pulling them together across the centre of the pot with the same colour.

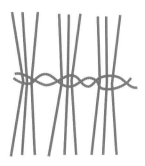

Garland

Using one strand of Au Ver à Soie Green 199, zigzag around the garland with little short stitches.

Work random colonial knots around the garland in one strand of Au Ver à Soie Purple 133.

Background

Photocopy the line drawings for the background (or trace them if you prefer).

Carefully cut out all the background pieces, then turn them over so that so that any remnants of the lines will be invisible, and glue small pieces of foam core to the back of each cut-out.

Arrange the pieces on the foam core background. When you are happy with the placement, glue the pieces down one at a time. Finish with a bow glued below the tree, made from a strip of 4-sheet card about 8 x ⅜ in (20 x 1 cm) folded as shown in the diagram.

shape the cardboard strip into a bow,
folding a $1/4$ in (6 mm) wide strip across the centre

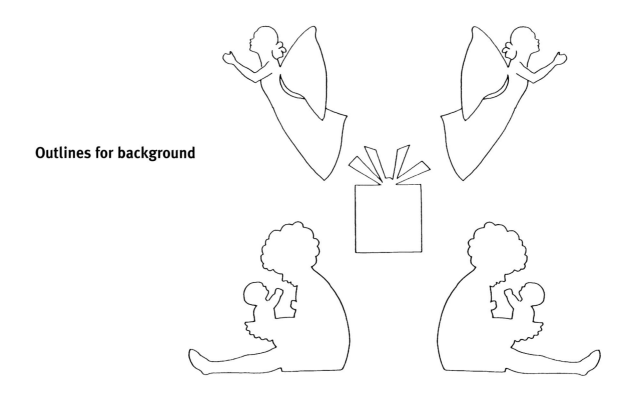

Outlines for background

Christmas Angel

ngel are supernatural beings in the image of man, their purpose being messengers of God. We think of angels mainly at Christmas, as decorations for table settings and to adorn the tops of trees. This angel is a Christmas angel, proclaiming God's goodwill towards man. It is embellished with a flourish of ribbon in a style reminiscent of baroque calligraphy. The colours are understatedly elegant in silver, gold and white.

Requirements

2 frames 12 ½ in (32 cm) square
organza to cover one frame
⅛ in (3 mm) white foam core for background and stage
Golden Threads: Silver Passing
Madeira Heavy Metal Art 9844: 30 6032
YLI Silk: Angel's Wings 113
7 mm white silk ribbon
pearls or pearl beads
cream and gold marbled paper

Stitches

Couching stitch, running stitch, satin stitch

Transferring the design

Make two frames 12 ½ inches (32 cm) square. Stretch organza onto one frame as detailed on page 21.

Transfer the design onto the framed organza. Centre the frame, organza side down, onto the pattern and trace with a soft black lead pencil or water-erasable pen (see page 21).

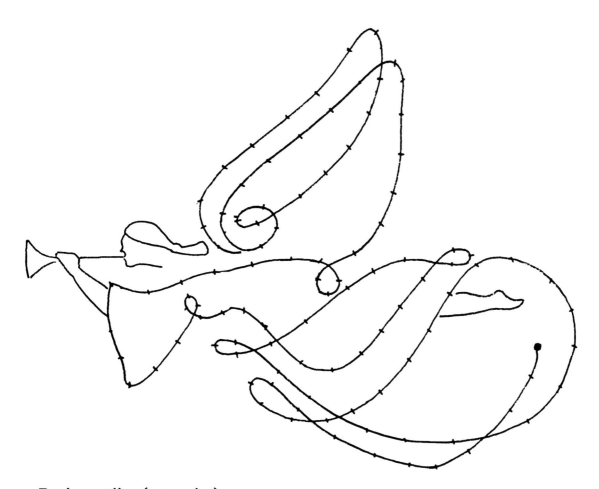

Tracing outline (same size)

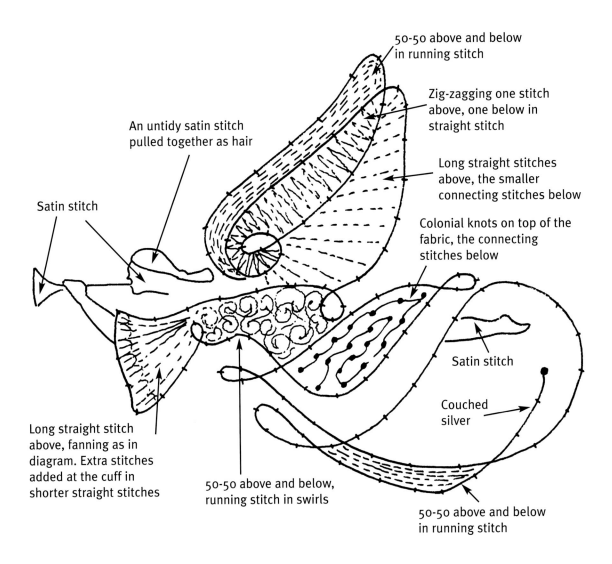

50-50 above and below
in running stitch

Zig-zagging one stitch
above, one below in
straight stitch

Long straight stitches
above, the smaller
connecting stitches below

An untidy satin stitch
pulled together as hair

Satin stitch

Colonial knots on top of the
fabric, the connecting
stitches below

Satin stitch

Couched
silver

Long straight stitch
above, fanning as in
diagram. Extra stitches
added at the cuff in
shorter straight stitches

50-50 above and below,
running stitch in swirls

50-50 above and below
in running stitch

Angel

Couch the silver cord in one length along the traced outline,
starting just behind the angel's head and finishing near the foot,
using one strand of YLI Silk Angel's Wings 113 as the sewing
thread. Begin and finish by taking the cord to the back with a
darning needle and sewing the end securely.

Satin-stitch the face, hands and feet in one strand of YLI Silk
Angel's Wings 113.
Following the diagram, fill in the various areas outlined by the
silver cord in different stitches in YLI Silk Angel's Wings 113. You
may find it helpful to refer to the photograph.

Work the hair and trumpet in satin stitch in one strand of
Madeira Gold.

Ribbon	Embellish the upper body and the bottom of the robe with folds of silk ribbon, using the photograph as a guide.
	In the folds around the bottom of the robe, sew in pearls or beads.
Background	Use a simple stage covered in marbled paper, available from wedding stationers or specialty paper shops.

Tree Ferns

Tree ferns (or man ferns, as they are sometimes known) are amongst the oldest species of plant life, prehistoric in their appearance and make-up. Coming from Tasmania, where they are abundant in the forests, I have plenty of opportunity to walk amongst these beautiful plants. From their bases in the leaf litter to the tips of their fronds they are classic in their design. However, nothing is more beautiful than the unfurling of the fronds. On each tree, like a time-lapse movie, the unfurling can be seen, from the furry brown fiddleheads beginning with little glimpses of green leaf to young fronds with slowly opening tips, still soft and crinkled.

Growing in the moss in the dappled light between the man ferns are colonies of smaller ferns with lacy leaves and minute detail. There is enough inspiration in a walk through a fern glade to last a lifetime.

http://www.view.com.au/dombrovskis/2-0.htmhttp:// www.discovertasmania.com.au/home/index.cfm?SiteID=107

Requirements
2 frames 12 ½ inches (32 cm) square
organza to cover one frame
⅛ in (3 mm) white foam core for background and stage
Madeira Silk 018: Fiddle Brown 2008, Fern Green 1312
green watercolour paint

Stitches
Running stitch, detached buttonhole, straight stitch, satin stitch

Transferring the design

Make two frames 12 ½ inches (32 cm) square. Stretch organza onto one frame as detailed on page 21.

Transfer the design onto the framed organza. Centre the frame, organza side down, onto the pattern and trace with a soft black lead pencil or water-erasable pen (see page 21). You may prefer to omit the leaflet outlines in the lower part of the design, merely indicating where each one joins the stem.

Tracing outline (same size)

Fiddleheads   Using one strand of Madeira Fiddle Brown 2008, work five rows of zigzag running stitch for each fiddle, starting from the bottom.

Smooth out the zigzags when going around the corner of the fiddlehead. Make sure that the divisions around the head are clearly defined, using a straight stitch distorted into a curve with a small catching stitch.

Using the photograph as a guide, fill in the segments of the fiddlehead with satin stitch. Take advantage of the gaps created as the satin stitch pulls the segments apart; the segments can be defined without leaving an actual gap.

Now, using one strand of Madeira Fern Green 1312, work running stitch between the brown zigzags, only up as far as the satin stitch. In the same thread, loosely lay a straight stitch into the valleys between the segments of the fiddleheads. In the middle of each fiddlehead create the suggestion of a leaf by working a detached buttonhole, still in the same thread.

To embroider the green twigs amongst the fiddleheads, work four long straight stitches side by side on top of the fabric in one strand of Madeira Fern Green 1312. For the curved twigs, bend the straight stitches with a couple of small catching stitches coming up from the back.

Along each twig, using one strand of Madeira Fiddle Brown 2006, work random straight stitches protruding from the green. These stitches should point upwards.

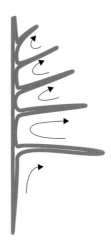

Fronds

Embroider the stems first, in one strand of Madeira Fiddle Brown 2006, working up one side and down the other, in a small running stitch. To minimise knots try to work in a loop, going out to the end of a branch and back to the main stem, then on to the next.

Using one strand of Madeira Fern Green 1407, work each leaflet with a cluster of four or five small straight stitches fanning out from the stem. Work from one leaflet to the other, in the same direction and manner as the branches. When moving to the next leaflet make a small stitch over the stem; this will both anchor the green thread in place and subtly tone the brown thread.

Background

Use a simple stage lightly and unevenly washed in green with watercolour or coloured pencil. To add a little texture, wrap four full strands of Madeira Fiddle Brown 2008 across the stage at the level of the bases of the fiddleheads.

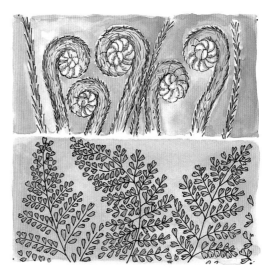

Peacock Feather

The peacock feather, most beautiful of all feathers, has inspired artists since the beginning of recorded history. Greek mythology says that the eyes of the feathers are the eyes of Argus, servant of the goddess Hera. In the Book of Kings we are told that the ships of Tarshish brought King Solomon peacocks from India every three years. Today these feathers are found on fabrics, wall coverings, jewellery and Tiffany lamps. Their shimmering metallic colours are an optical illusion created by the play of light. I have tried to replicate the look through the use of a variety of metallic threads.

Requirements

2 frames 12 ½ in (32 cm) square

organza to cover one frame

⅛ in (3 mm) white foam core for background and stage

Golden Threads Couching Thread: Copper 371, Cedar Green 317, Black Opal 317

Golden Threads Silver Passing

Gumnut Yarns: Argus Purple 299

Madeira Jewel Art: Hologram Pink 9843

Madeira Heavy Metal Art 9844: 30 6032

Madeira Silk 018: Tarshish Blue 1007, King Solomon Gold 0105, Hera Green 1214, Indian Spice 2008

large quill (found object)

Stitches

Couching, long stitch, running stitch

Transferring the design

Make two frames 12 ½ inches (32 cm) square. Stretch organza onto one frame as detailed on page 21.

Transfer the design onto the framed organza. Centre the frame, organza side down, onto the pattern and trace with a soft black lead pencil or water-erasable pen (see page 21).

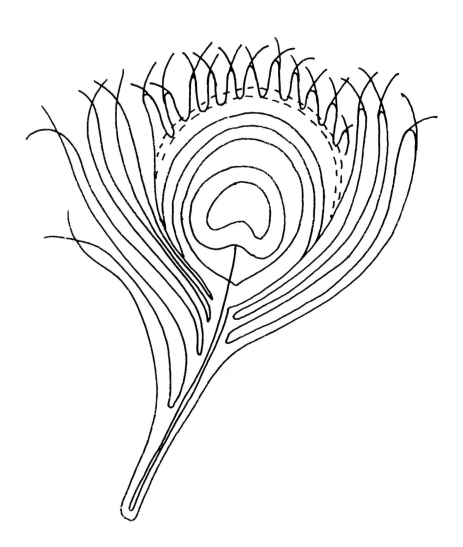

Tracing outline (same size)

Feather

Refer to the photograph for guidance in this project.

Couch the kidney shape in the centre of the eye in Black Opal, using Tarshish Blue 1007 as the sewing thread.

Couch Cedar Green around the Black Opal, again using Tarshish Blue 1007 as the sewing thread.

Radiate straight stitches around the green eye in Madeira Indian Spice 2008.

Place a strand of Madeira King Solomon Gold 0105 and a strand of Madeira Hera Green 1214 in the needle and work straight stitches radiating out from the Indian Spice.

Using Madeira Jewel Hologram Pink, work an arc of short straight stitches crossing over the centres of the threads in the green and gold band.

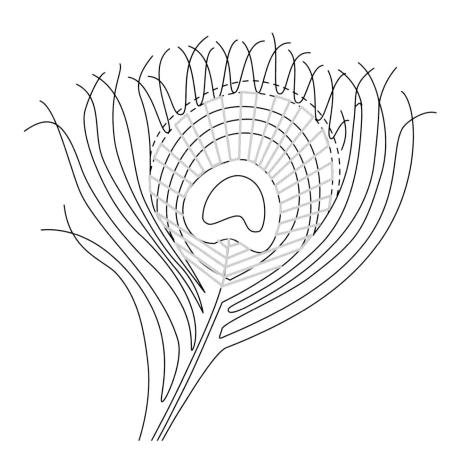

Next, using a single strand of Madeira Gold, work long straight stitches, from the edge of the central Cedar Green eye, over the bands of Indian Spice, King Solomon Gold, Hera Green and Hologram Pink, to the outer edge of the rounded shape.

Beginning at the right side of the base of the feather, couch down the copper cord directly from the reel, using Madeira Tarshish Blue 1007 as the sewing thread, to form the outer wispy part of the feather. Work without cutting the copper cord, changing direction with sharp turns.

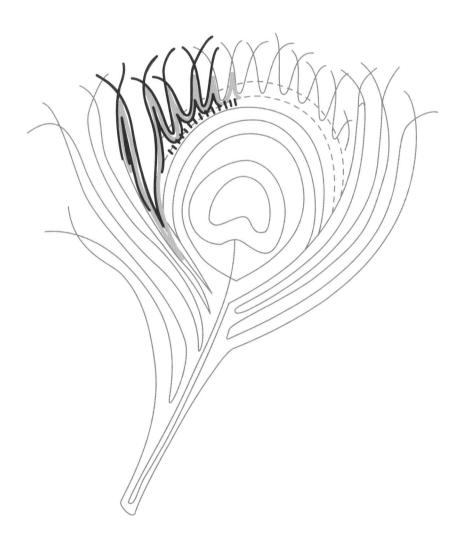

To add softness to the copper cord and disguise the sharp turns, work a running stitch in Gumnut Argus Purple 299 on either side. Use stitches of equal length above and below the organza.

Couch a length of Silver Passing up the centre vein of the feather to the edge of the band of Cedar Green; couch a second length alongside it, taking this one up to the edge of the mixed Hera Green and King Solomon Gold band. Use a single strand of Tarshish Blue 1007 as the sewing thread.

Background

Use either a simple stage for the background or, as I have done, an abstract arrangement of foam core rectangles of different shapes and heights. I finished the background with a section of a quill shaft from a peacock feather sewn to a long foam core rectangle painted a soft dark blue.

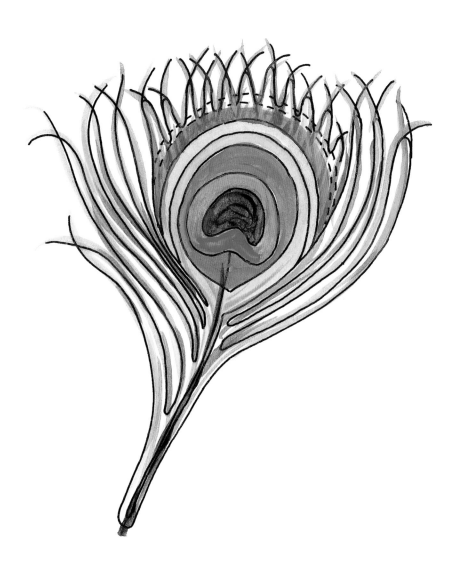

Design Suggestions

The unworked designs in this section have been chosen to inspire you to make your own interpretations of different aspects of this type of embroidery. I would love to see what you do with them. If you would like to send me a digital photo I would be delighted to share your work with others on my website. Don't feel that these designs must be worked as I have suggested—my notes are only intended to get you thinking. Happy stitching.

Cyclamen

Treat this design very delicately. Work from the centre of the design out towards the edges, using less detail as you move further out. Work more detail in the leaves, using two shades of blue-green, and perhaps silver for the white veins. Work the stems in a deep burgundy pink. Finish with a simple stage.

Winter rose

The winter rose is a very subtle blend of clear yellow-greens,
blushed with a secondary colour of dusty pink. Detail the flowers
and parts of the leaves, fading the leaves out at the edges. A
yellow-green shade, of white stage, (White is never simply white it
has a foundation colour, in this case it is recommended it be yellow-
green) placed on a darker green would add to the overall subtlety
of the work. Use the frame and mount to complement and
accentuate the shading in the work.

Orchid

The orchid could be worked in any tropical colour scheme. Work the flower first, being creative with your colour blends, and adding highlights of gold or pearl. Work the leaves in strong pure greens. Following the shapes of the leaves, cut leaves from light white card for the background, offset and slightly bend to create a shadow.

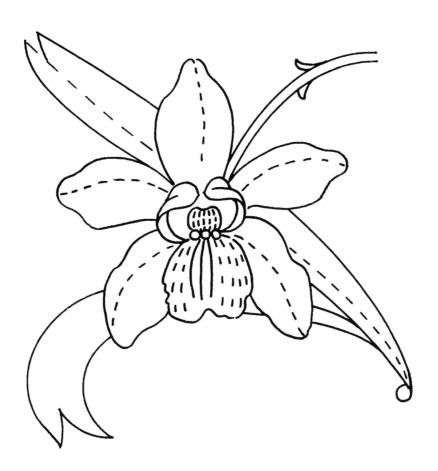

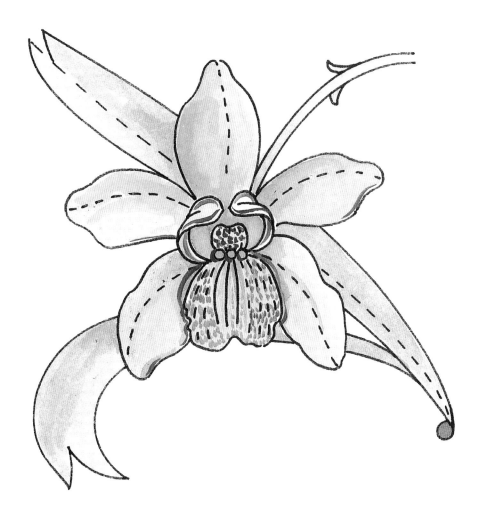

Poppy

A feast of light and shade … work the flower first in appropriate poppy colours. Work the left-hand leaf in a greenish white, and the dark shadowy leaves in the background in a green-grey. Outline the foreground leaf in green-grey to distinguish the form. Highlight the centre of the flower with glass beads. Echo the leaf shape in the background, either as a paper cut-out or in watercolours.

Lily

Work the back three petals directly on the organza. Work the front three as detached petals in a hoop, and cut them out, in similar manner to the wings of the butterfly on page 132. Use a couching thread to form the gentle curves of the stems. A thin silk cushion with a delicate edging, the size of a simple stage, would make an interesting background.

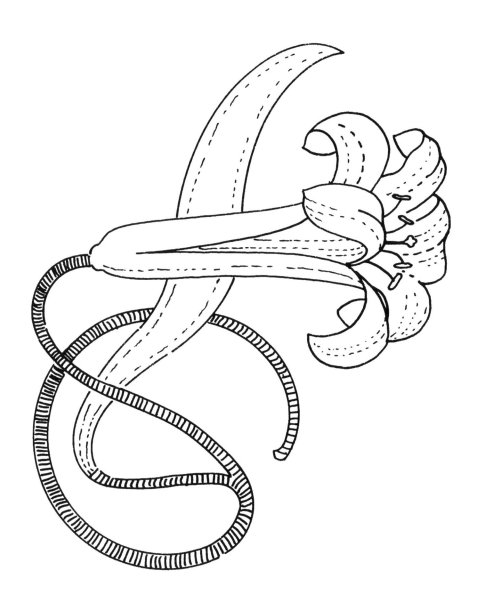

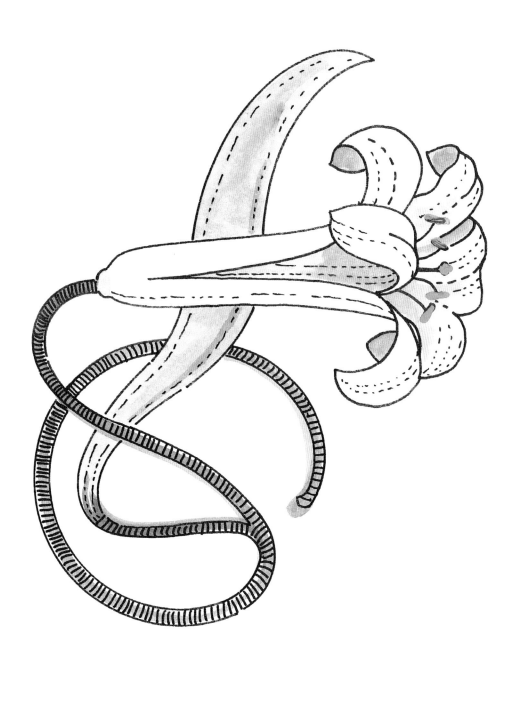

Lily-of-the-valley

I suggest you use silk for this project, as the sheen of silk suits the character of this flower. Use colours ranging from white to magnolia for the flowers, and a deep spring green for the leaves. A delicate silk ribbon threaded through the organza and tied in a bow at the base of the flower would add a new dimension to the work.

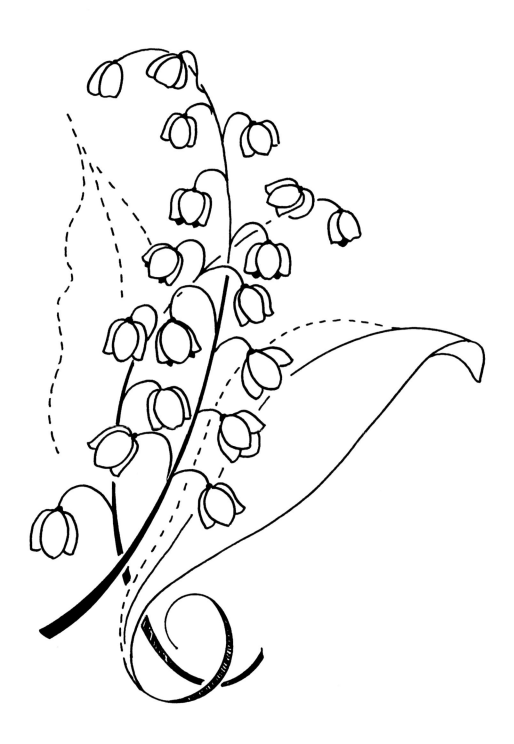

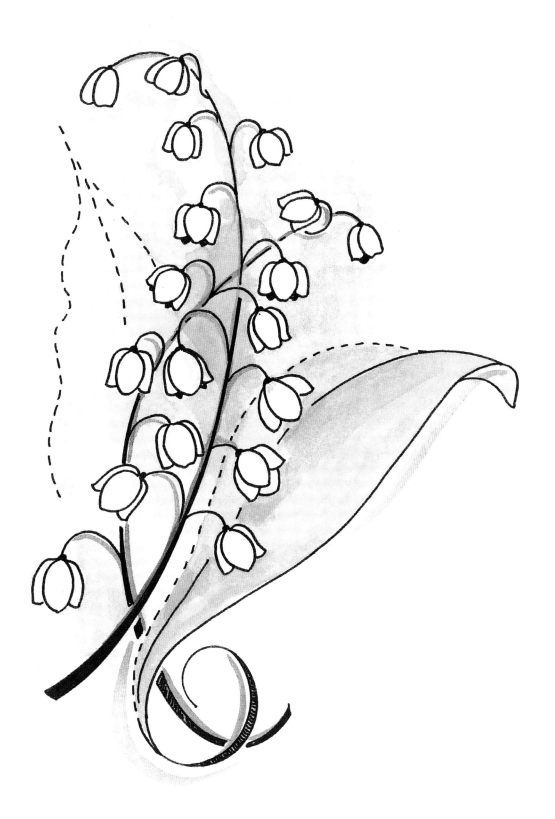

Tulip

Work the tulip in traditional bright clear colours. Work the petals in a running stitch mainly on the top of the organza. When blending, alternate the colours, first 50/50, 40/60, 30/70 and so on, until the colour change is made. The leaf could be worked in a similar manner to the agapanthus leaf on page 73. For the stage you might like to copy some botanical information on tulips, printing it in a light grey.

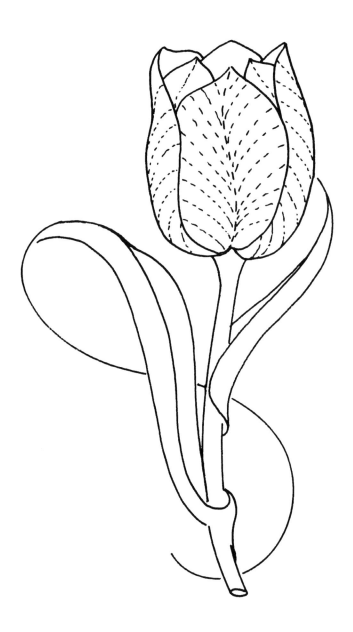

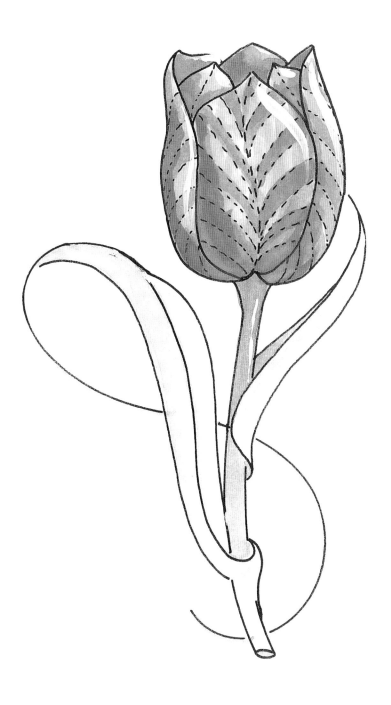

Fuchsia

The nature of the fuchsia lends itself to being heavily worked in satin stitch in the main part of the design, getting lighter towards the outer edges. The second flower might be worked all in shadow satin stitch to create a slightly out-of-focus look, like a flower in the background of a photograph. A simple stage would be sufficient to set off the work.

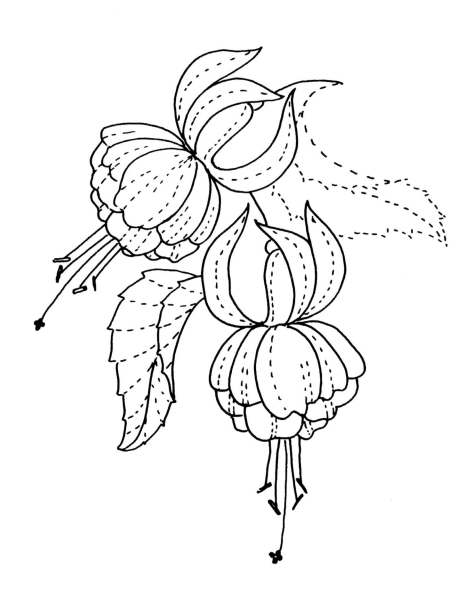

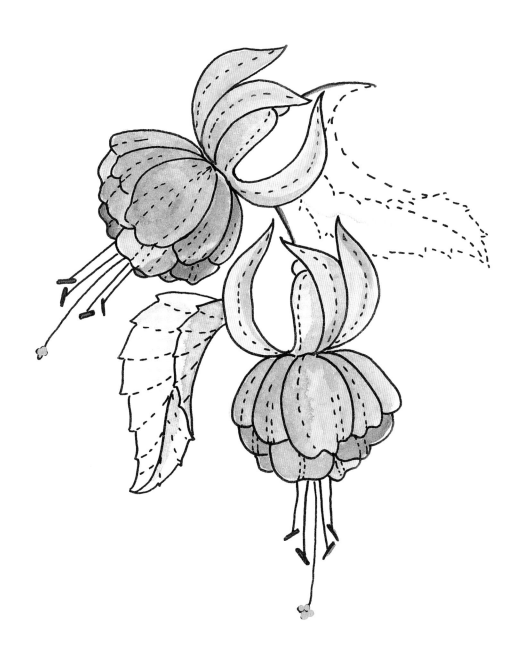

Arum lily

There are many colours in this flower today. Apart from the shape they all have another thing in common—the colours are delicately blushed onto a satiny white. If you are adventurous you might like to dye your own thread. Silk is very easy to dye with silk hobby dyes, using a microwave oven. Mix up a colour such as pink, very well diluted, in a mug. Loosely wind about 5 metres of silk into a hank and submerge it in the dye. Bring the contents of the mug to the boil, submerging the silk several times, as it will rise to the surface. Start with a mixture that is almost clear, for it is always better to double dip or add extra colour than to start out too dark.

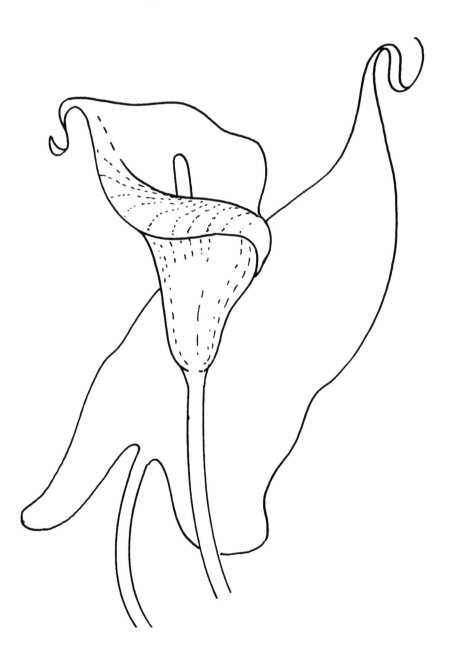

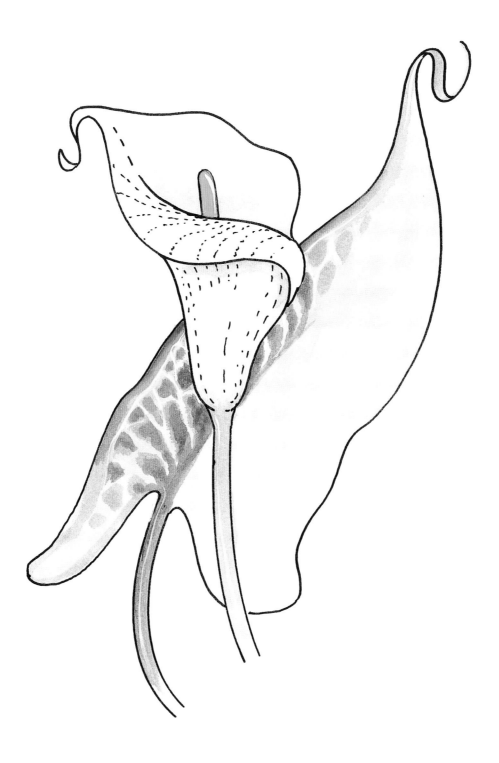

Iris

This design would lend itself well to the use of threads in variegated colour, a style of thread I have not specified elsewhere in the book as the best are usually available from small companies that do not trade worldwide. In this flower you have the opportunity to use many different stitches; some parts might be done in stumpwork (dimensional embroidery).

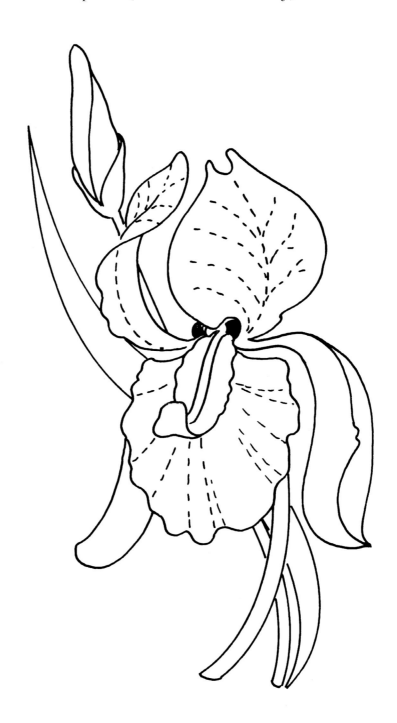

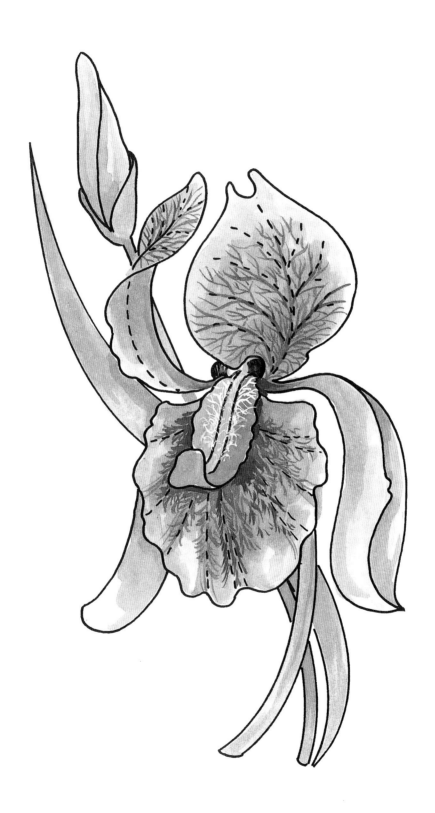

Wild rose

You might treat this piece in similar fashion to the blackberries on page 57. It would also work well with two screens, as were used for the Lovely Wren on page 75. In this case you would work one screen following the diagram, the second as a reverse image off-centred from the first. This will give the design a three-dimensional aspect. Use a simple stage to highlight and frame the design.

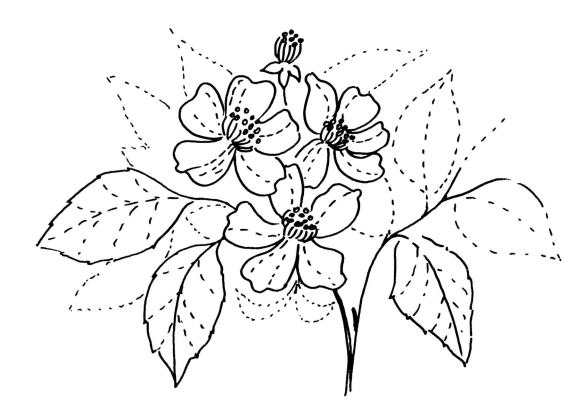

Boy — "Before the War"

I have chosen the last four designs to be worked in the same manner as Little Bo-Peep on page 121.

Girl — "Studio Portrait"

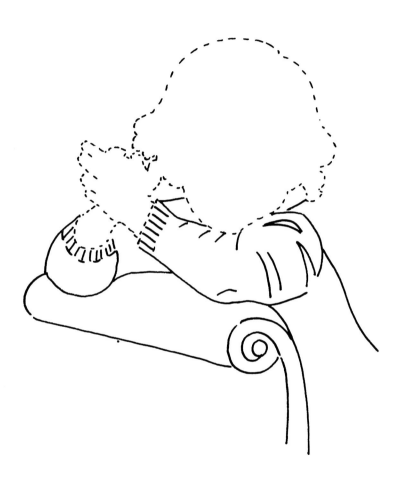

Lady — "Wedding Day"

Man — "The Bushman"

Distributors

Supplier of Gary Clarke Designs kits, books and threads

Gary Clarke Designs
Po Box 787
Launceston Tasmania 7250 Australia
Fax: 61 3 6334 1525
Email: stitching.heirlooms@microtech.com.au
Web: http://www.garyclarkedesigns.com

Madeira Threads

Penguin Threads
35 Mount Street
Prahran Victoria 3181 Australia
Phone: 61 3 9529 4400
Fax: 61 3 9525 1172
Email: info@penguin-threads.com.au
Web: http://www.penguin-threads.com.au

Madeira USA (Headquarters)
30 Bayside Ct.
P.O. Box 6068
Laconia NH   03246 U.S.A.
800 225 3001
Tel: 603 528 2944
Fax: 603 528 4264
Email: Madeirausa@aol.com

Au Ver a Soie & Golden Threads Australia

Ristal Threads
Tel: 61 2 6241 2293
Fax: 61 2 6241 8382
Email: ristal@austarmetro.com.au

Au Ver a Soie & Golden Threads USA

Access Commodities
Po Box 1355
Terrell Texas 75160 U.S.A.
Tel: 972 563 3313
Fax: 972 563 3330

Delica Beads

Maria George Pty Ltd
Phone: 61 3 9650 1151
Fax: 61 3 9650 5318
Email: mariag@mariageorge.com.au
Web: http://www.mariageorge.com.au

Rajmahal Threads

Rajmahal Threads Australia
1 Anderson Street
Bendigo Victoria 3550 Australia
Tel: 61 3 5441 7787
Fax: 61 3 5441 7959
Email: rajinfo@ozemail.com.au
Web: http://www.ramjahal.com.au

Rajmahal Threads USA
For distributors internationally
please refer to the above web site

Gumnut Yarns

Gumnut Yarns Australia
Po Box 519
Mudgee NSW 2850 Australia
Tel: 61 2 6374 2661
Fax: 61 2 6374 2771
Email: info@gumnutyarns.com
Web: http://www.gumnutyarns.com

Gumnut Yarns USA
Custom House of Needle Art
LLC 154 Weir Street
Glastonburg   CT   06033   U.S.A.
Tel/fax: 860 633 2950

YLI Silks

YLI Silks Australia
Cotton on Creations
Po Box 318
Blackheath   NSW   2785   Australia
Tel: 61 2 4787 6588
Fax: 61 2 4787 6544
Email: cottononcreations@bigpond.com.au

YLI Silks USA
Quilters Resource
Tel: 773 278 5695
Fax: 775 278 1348

Checker Distributors
Tel: 419 893 3636
Fax: 419 893 2422

Blue Bolt Fabrics

(Merrilyn Heazlewood)
107 Liverpool Street
Hobart Tasmania 7250 Australia
Tel/fax: 61 3 6234 4468